PROJECT BOOK

Simon Cupit

Shaftesbury Road, Cambridge CB2 8EA, United Kingdom

One Liberty Plaza, 20th Floor, New York, NY 10006, USA

477 Williamstown Road, Port Melbourne, VIC 3207, Australia

314–321, 3rd Floor, Plot 3, Splendor Forum, Jasola District Centre, New Delhi – 110025, India

103 Penang Road, #05-06/07, Visioncrest Commercial, Singapore 238467

José Abascal, 56–10, 28003 Madrid, Spain

Cambridge University Press & Assessment is a department of the University of Cambridge.

We share the University's mission to contribute to society through the pursuit of education, learning and research at the highest international levels of excellence.

www.cambridge.org
Information on this title: www.cambridge.org/9781108726627

First published 2020

20 19 18 17 16 15 14 13 12 11 10 9 8 7

Printed in Great Britain by Ashford Colour Press Ltd.

A catalogue record for this publication is available from the British Library

ISBN 978-1-108-72662-7 Own it! Project Book Level 1
ISBN 978-84-1322-011-6 Collaborate Project Book Level 1

Additional resources for this publication at www.cambridge.org/ownit/resources

Cambridge University Press & Assessment has no responsibility for the persistence or accuracy of URLs for external or third-party internet websites referred to in this publication, and does not guarantee that any content on such websites is, or will remain, accurate or appropriate. Information regarding prices, travel timetables, and other factual information given in this work is correct at the time of first printing but Cambridge University Press & Assessment does not guarantee the accuracy of such information thereafter.

CONTENTS

AN INTRODUCTION TO PROJECT WORK

Welcome back to school! Your new class of excited, nervous students is waiting for you. Each one of them comes from a unique background.

Have they had the opportunity to experience project work before? We know that successful language learning takes place when students are able to communicate real meaning. Project work provides multiple possibilities for this. By working together towards a goal, students can become more motivated, as well as develop key communication, critical-thinking and decision-making skills.

This book will guide you on how to make the most of your projects, and help your students work successfully both in and out of the classroom.

What is project work?

Imagine you and your class have just finished Unit 5 (*What's your style?*). Your students have learned vocabulary for clothes and accessories and practised functional language for buying these items. How can you review and build on this topic? You are in luck! Each unit is accompanied by a project. In this case, your students choose a style of clothing that they like and make a lookbook about it. Groups find pictures for the different sections and create a book to describe what people are wearing.

This is project work: students being responsible for their work and making decisions together. There is a realistic final objective and a series of stages to follow, where groups can explore how to achieve their goals. The final aim is always a presentation stage. > Presentation ideas p18 Your role is to help this happen. As a result, students learn by doing and have a good experience to look back on.

Throughout the project work process, students develop a number of **life skills**. They learn to:

Create new ideas

Question actively

Use social skills

Think critically

Work together

Create

BENEFITS AND ADVANTAGES OF PROJECT WORK

✓ Personal advantages

- encourages **creativity** by promoting **different ways of thinking**
- increases **motivation** through challenge
- develops **independence** and a **sense of responsibility**
- increases natural **curiosity**
- improves **self-knowledge** through **self-evaluation**
- improves **communication skills** through teamwork
- involves family and friends in the **learning process**
- improves **interpersonal** relationships
- develops **life skills**

✓ Academic advantages

- allows teachers to deal with **mixed-ability** classes
- motivates whole-team / cooperation / group work and promotes chances to **learn from one another**
- develops **planning** and **organisational skills**
- permits a 'flipped classroom' approach
- **helps learning** through research and opportunities for deep thinking
- increases opportunities to **integrate cross-curricular** and **cultural topics**
- encourages **peer teaching** and **correction**
- enables students with **different learning styles** to help one another

✓ Language learning

- provides opportunities to **use language naturally**
- integrates all **four skills** (reading, writing, listening and speaking)
- allows for the use of **self- and peer-evaluation language**
- encourages research and **use of English out of the class**
- is learner-centred: students **learn language from one another**
- practises both **fluency** and **accuracy** through different types of presentations

Project work and the Cambridge Life Competencies Framework

How can we prepare our students to succeed in a changing world? We see the need to help students develop transferable skills, to work with people from around the globe, to think creatively, analyse sources critically and communicate their views. However, how can we balance the development of these skills with the demands of the language curriculum?

Cambridge have developed the Cambridge Life Competencies Framework. This Framework reinforces project work, helping teachers recognise and assess the many transferable skills that project work develops, alongside language learning.

The Framework provides different levels of detail, from six Competencies to specific Can Do Statements. The Competencies are supported by three foundation layers.

Critical Thinking	Creative Thinking	Collaboration	Communication	Learning to Learn	Social Responsibilities

EMOTIONAL DEVELOPMENT AND WELLBEING	DIGITAL LITERACY	DISCIPLINE KNOWLEDGE

It then defines specific Core Areas. For example, here are the Core Areas for Collaboration.

Taking personal responsibility for own contribution to a group task.	Listening respectfully and responding constructively to others' contributions.	Managing the sharing of tasks in a project.	Working towards a resolution related to a task.

Then, there is a Can Do Statement for each Core Area. These will differ depending on the age of the students.

Competency
Collaboration

↓

Core Area
Managing the sharing of tasks in a project.

↓

Can Do Statements

- Follows the instructions for a task and alerts others when not following them.
- Explains reasons for suggestions and contributions.
- Takes responsibility for completing tasks as part of a larger project.

For more information, go to:
cambridge.org/elt

Level 1 Projects	Competency	Core Area	Can Do Statements
The culture project: a poster 👆 Teacher's Resource Bank Unit 1	Creative Thinking	Creating new content from own ideas or other resources	*Illustrates a new poster with unique symbols or persuasive language; Responds imaginatively to contemporary events and ideas.*
	Collaboration	Managing the sharing of tasks in a project	*Works with others to plan and execute class projects; Ensures that all members have a role in group activities.*
The maths project: a class survey 📖 Student's Book pp30–31	Communication	Using appropriate language and register for context	*Knows how to present points clearly and persuasively; Uses language for effect (exaggerations).*
	Critical Thinking	Evaluating ideas, arguments and options	*Identifies evidence and its reliability; Gives reasons for an argument's plausibility.*
The culture project: a haiku 👆 Teacher's Resource Bank Unit 3	Learning to Learn	Practical skills for participating in learning	*Organises notes systematically; Uses notes to construct original output.*
	Social Responsibilities	Taking active roles including leadership	*Sets strategies and plans; Shows confidence in speaking in public (e.g. to present a project).*
The art project: a food truck 📖 Student's Book pp54–55	Creative Thinking	Using newly created content to solve problems	*Employs new ideas and content in solving a task or activity; Makes an assignment original by adding new angles.*
	Collaboration	Taking personal responsibility for own contributions	*Follows the instructions for a task; Explains reasons for their suggestions and contributions.*
The culture project: a lookbook 👆 Teacher's Resource Bank Unit 5	Communication	Participating with appropriate confidence and clarity	*Speaks with suitable fluency; Uses facial expressions and eye contact appropriately.*
	Learning to Learn	Taking control of own learning	*Identifies helpful resources for their learning; Uses a learner's dictionary and other reference resources.*
The PE project: an information leaflet 📖 Student's Book pp78–79	Communication	Participating with appropriate confidence and clarity	*Develops a clear description with a logical sequence of points; Uses a number of cohesive devices to link sentences into clear, coherent discourse.*
	Critical Thinking	Synthesising ideas and information	*Selects key points from diverse sources to create a new account and/or argument.*
The culture project: a scrapbook 👆 Teacher's Resource Bank Unit 7	Social Responsibilities	Understanding and describing own and others' cultures	*Accepts others and shows respect for cultural difference; Understands the contributions of different cultures to their own lives.*
	Creative Thinking	Creating new content from own ideas or other resources	*Writes or tells an original story, given prompts or without prompts; Makes up own 'what if' activities and brings others in.*
The history project: an interview 📖 Student's Book pp102–103	Critical Thinking	Evaluating ideas, arguments and options	*Distinguishes between fact and opinion; Identifies assumptions and inferences in an argument.*
	Collaboration	Listening respectfully and responding constructively to others' contributions or activities	*Is ready to justify, adapt and abandon a proposal in response to others' queries and contributions; Listens to, acknowledges different points of view, respectfully.*
The culture project: a webpage 👆 Teacher's Resource Bank Unit 9	Creative Thinking	Participating in creative activities	*Encourages group members to make activities more original; Participates in activities that include creative thinking.*
	Learning to Learn	Taking control of own learning	*Finds sources of information and help; Reviews vocabulary regularly and systematically.*

HOW TO USE THE PROJECT BOOK

See learning outcomes, as well as the skills students will develop and the resources and evaluation tools you may wish to use.

Manage student roles and responsibilities.

Monitor and check the skills that project work develops, mapped to the Cambridge Life Competencies Framework.

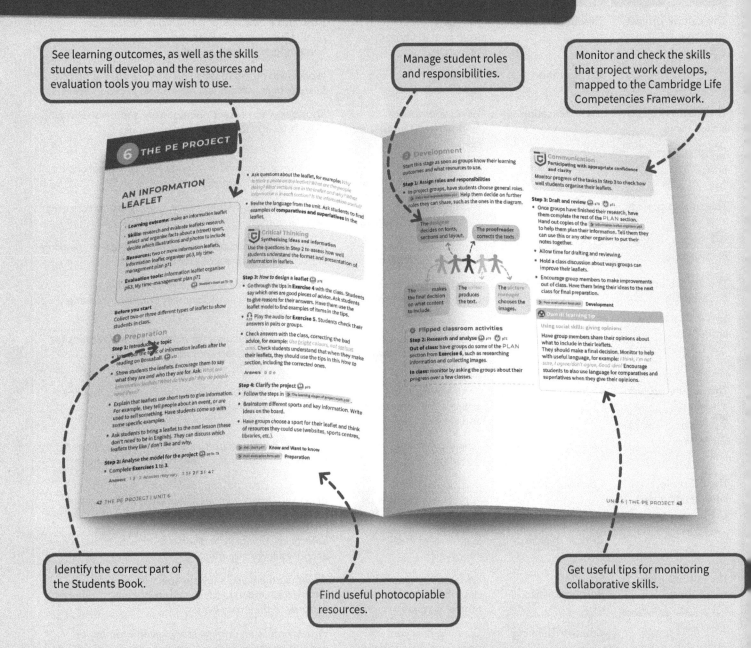

Identify the correct part of the Students Book.

Find useful photocopiable resources.

Get useful tips for monitoring collaborative skills.

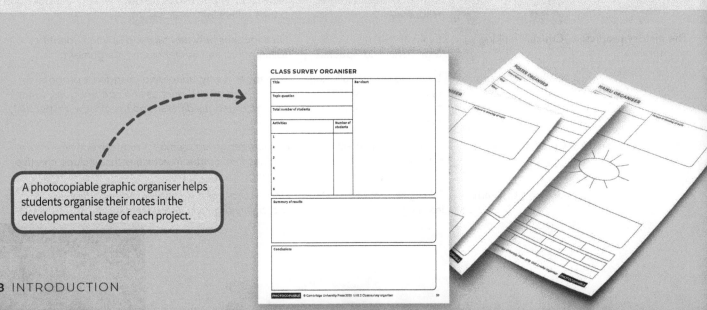

A photocopiable graphic organiser helps students organise their notes in the developmental stage of each project.

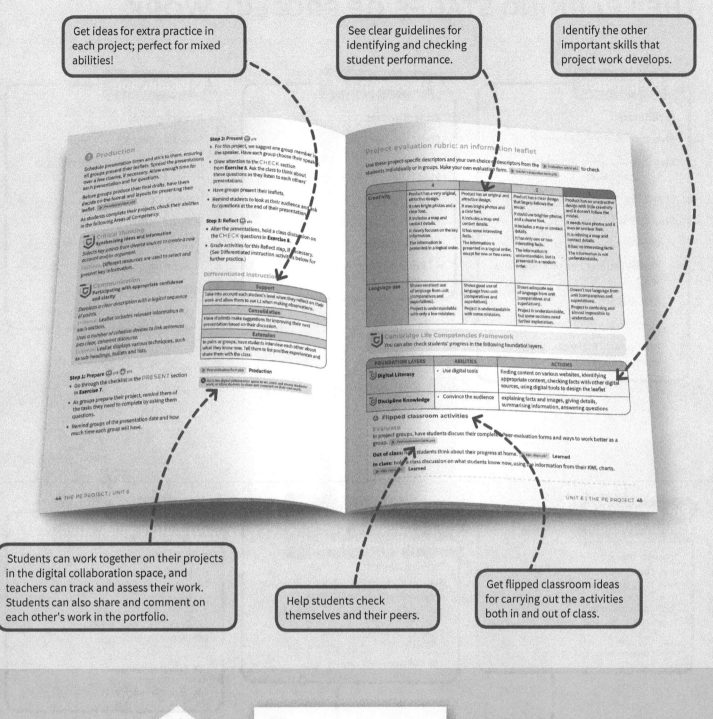

Get ideas for extra practice in each project; perfect for mixed abilities!

See clear guidelines for identifying and checking student performance.

Identify the other important skills that project work develops.

Students can work together on their projects in the digital collaboration space, and teachers can track and assess their work. Students can also share and comment on each other's work in the portfolio.

Help students check themselves and their peers.

Get flipped classroom ideas for carrying out the activities both in and out of class.

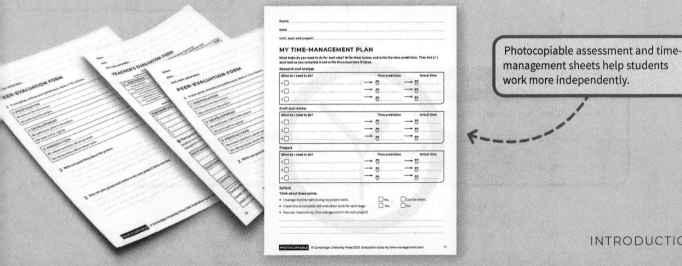

Photocopiable assessment and time-management sheets help students work more independently.

THE LEARNING STAGES OF PROJECT WORK

1 Preparation

Facilitators

Step 1: Introduce the topic

Step 2: Analyse the model for the project

Step 3: Go through the *How to* tips

Step 4: Clarify the project

- Organise groups
- Review the learning outcomes and skills
- Brainstorm ideas
- Focus on key information
- Have groups make decisions about content

2 Development

Project groups

Step 1: Assign roles and responsibilities

Step 2: Research and analyse

Step 3: Draft and review

- Put together work
- Peer-correct
- Express opinions and make choices

3 Production

Project groups

Step 1: Prepare

- Decide how the project will look and who will speak
- Practise

Step 2: Present

- Take turns presenting
- Ask questions and give feedback

Step 3: Reflect

- Discuss all stages of the process

Pre-evaluation (self-evaluation)

Tools for students:
KWL chart, My learning diary, Peer-evaluation form

Tools for teachers:
Teacher's evaluation form

> **>** Evaluation tools pp67–70

Formative evaluation (self-evaluation, peer-evaluation, observation)

Tools for students:
KWL chart, My learning diary, graphic organisers, Peer-evaluation form

Tools for teachers:
Teacher's evaluation form

> **>** Evaluation tools pp67–70

Formative and summative evaluation

Tools for students:
KWL chart, My learning diary, Peer-evaluation form

Tools for teachers:
Teacher's evaluation form, Evaluation rubric

> **>** Evaluation tools pp67–70

> **>** Evaluation rubric p21

Reflection (you and students)

1. Have *student-to-student*, *student-to-teacher* and *teacher-to-student* discussions on evaluation grades.

2. Identify areas for improvement in future projects using the Evaluation tools.

> **>** Evaluation p20

L1 IN PROJECT WORK

Many teachers believe that the only way for students to learn English effectively is by using it at all times in class. They feel that any time students spend using their own language is a missed opportunity.

Do you allow L1 use in your classroom? If you do, don't worry: there is little data to support the above idea (Kerr, 2016)[1]. In fact, there are occasions when allowing students to use L1 is positive. This is particularly true of project work.

We can use L1 in different steps of the project cycle. Take *Clarify the project* as an example (Preparation stage, Step 4). If students fail to understand the project's objectives, they won't carry it out properly. Allowing L1 use is not a 'missed opportunity' here. It ensures a richer project experience.

Of course, this doesn't mean you should use students' own language *all* of the time. You have to consider factors like age, level, the difficulty of the project and its outcomes. The question is not *if* you should use own language, but *when*, *how* and *how much*.

At Level 1, we suggest you allow own-language use for explanations, wider discussions, reflection and analysis, while encouraging English for research and presentation.

Tips for L1 use

- Set rules for when students can use L1.
- Encourage groups to monitor their own-language use and explore English equivalents.
- Allow students 'own-language moments' (Kerr, 2014: 26–29)[2], such as preparing for speaking activities. Remember that the students' goal is to produce English in the Production stage of project work.

OL = Own language, E = English, [grey] shows suggested language

THE LEARNING STAGES OF PROJECT WORK		
1 Preparation	OL	E
Introducing and discussing the topic		
Analysing the model for the project		
Going through the *How to* tips		
Clarifying the project		
2 Development	OL	E
Assigning roles and responsibilities		
Researching and analysing		
Drafting and reviewing		
3 Production	OL	E
Preparing the final presentation		
Presenting the project		
Reflecting on the process		

[1] Kerr, Philip (2016). 'The learner's own language. Explorations' in *English Language and Linguistics*. 3.1:1–7.
[2] Kerr, Philip (2014). *Translation and Own-language Activities*. Cambridge: Cambridge University Press.

MIXED ABILITIES IN PROJECT WORK

How can you teach in ways that suit each type of learner? Projects offer a great advantage in this area, as students can explore different ways of completing them.

Mixed-ability classes can depend on individual differences such as motivation, ability, age and experience. Allow your students to express their ideas in different ways, and remember that no one will be happy with a project that is too difficult or too easy.

Studies have shown that adolescence is the best time for instructed language learning. Teenagers are faster at learning and are ready to understand and use rules (DeKeyser, 2010)[1]. Your activities should reflect this, which means getting to know your students and their differences in the following four areas:

Cognitive maturity	**Proficiency**	**Interests**	**Learning preferences**
Your students' ages and experiences affect their ability to understand and follow instructions.	Every member of your class will have a different language level.	Teenagers have a wide variety of interests and skills.	Everyone has different learning preferences, such as reading, taking notes, asking questions, listening, moving around, or watching videos.
Adapt instructions according to level and avoid complicated words and phrases with beginners and elementary students.	Make sure tasks involve an appropriate degree of difficulty and are suitably challenging. Provide the levels of support needed.	Allow students to take roles within a project that help them develop their personal interests and relate to the main task. Encourage them to expand their knowledge.	Use a variety of learning styles in your classroom, such as visual, aural, verbal, physical or logical.

The roles of the facilitator

Give feedback

Is it a mouse?

Ask for and give reasons

Why? Because …

Encourage participation

What do you think?

Listen actively

That's interesting! Really?

---

[1] DeKeyser, R., Alfi-Shabtay, I., & Ravid, D. (2010). 'Cross-linguistic evidence for the nature of age effects in second language acquisition.' *Applied Psycholinguistics*, 31(3), 413–438.

Classroom suggestions

Challenge

Suggestion

Challenge	Suggestion
When working in groups, stronger students solve the problems, while others stay quiet.	Allow time for 'think, pair, share' activities, where students think individually first, discuss ideas with a partner, then share with another pair.
When weaker students are put in groups according to ability, they become labelled as 'less proficient', which affects their motivation and self-esteem.	Change groups to make sure all students benefit and contribute in different contexts.
High-ability students do not feel challenged.	Give extension work and higher-level input.
Weaker students do not complete tasks.	Give additional support and adapted activities.

Differentiated instruction

We provide a specific suggestion for differentiated instruction in each project.
Each one has three categories:

1 *Support* activities help students to better understand the tasks and concepts

2 *Consolidation* activities reinforce what students are learning

3 *Extension* activities provide additional challenges for more proficient students.

1 PREPARATION		
Support	**Consolidation**	**Extension**
Suggest ways to record and keep notes. Extend time limits. Give specific goals related to competencies.	Have students organise ideas. Provide specific tasks to improve competencies. Give extra roles and responsibilities.	Suggest alternative ideas. Focus on additional competencies. Set additional goals.

2 DEVELOPMENT		
Support	**Consolidation**	**Extension**
Provide more examples of models. Suggest sources for research. Give essential information that helps with students' roles. Ask specific questions about findings.	Analyse different models. Have students share opinions. Make additional notes of findings. Check sources. Give extra responsibility in line with roles.	Produce another model for the project. Analyse opinions. Look for different points of view. Allow for peer-teaching.

3 PRODUCTION		
Support	**Consolidation**	**Extension**
Check level-appropriate participation during presentation. Allow feedback in own language. Suggest ways to improve.	Encourage feedback in English. Have students discuss self-evaluation. Encourage suggestions for ways to improve.	Give all feedback and evaluation in English. Have students interview each other about what they learned. Encourage suggestions for ways to improve.

TIME MANAGEMENT IN PROJECT WORK

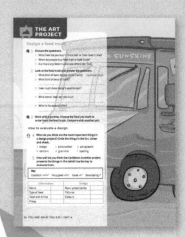

① Be prepared

Take a look at the project before you start the unit.

② Divide the project into smaller tasks

Every project is made of a number of smaller tasks, such as research, preparation, organising notes and brainstorming. Ask yourself:

- *How long will each task take?*
- *Can the task be done in class or out of class?*
- *At what stage of the unit can students complete each step?*
- *What language do they need?*

By approaching the project this way, you will see that the steps may not take up too much class time.

③ Prioritise and set short-term goals

Think about how the project groups can best use class time. Should they brainstorm, draw pictures or organise sentences? Be clear about what you want the groups to achieve by the end of each session.

It is important that groups present their projects when they expect to do so. It can be demotivating if you run out of time before they present.

④ Help students plan out-of-class assignments

Ensure the groups understand that the out-of-class tasks are just as important as the in-class ones when preparing a project. Set goals and give time limits. Encourage them to use their My time-management plans when you see this icon: ⏰

> My time-management plan p71

⑤ Be flexible between projects

How much time you give students for each task will vary from project to project. It may depend on factors such as previous knowledge, level of language difficulty or access to information.

⑥ Set a time for the presentation

Make sure you allow sufficient class time for the presentation step, including its evaluation. If the steps leading to the final product have been distributed and completed in an organised way, it's likely there will be more time for presenting it.

CHALLENGES AND IMPLICATIONS

The first year of secondary school coincides with important social, emotional and physiological changes. Many students at this age still prefer to work alone and it may take time for them to feel comfortable working in groups.

New secondary students will also have to adjust to their new environment. The year before, they were the oldest students in primary ... but now, they are suddenly among the youngest.

What are some changes and challenges to expect?

Change	Challenge
Academic: new subjects, new ways of working (less guided), different (more) teachers	organising time, planning when to study, doing homework, working in groups for projects
Environment: different building	overcoming fear after years in same school, getting to know new environment
Social: new people (some students might not know anyone)	adjusting to new groups, dealing with peer pressure
Self growth: physiological, emotional and moral changes	developing self-identity, thinking for themselves
Personal: more nervous about personal issues	sharing personal problems

All these changes and their challenges have implications for how to use project work in your classroom. You can encourage successful collaboration by:

- describing how you are going to organise your classes

- explaining how much guidance you will give, and your expectations

- making students feel excited about their new environment (showing them the computer room, library, etc.)

- getting to know the group and observing group dynamics

- organising group work from the start

- making sure no one is alone

- developing different skills through different ways of working (e.g. reflection, peer-evaluation, listening to others)

- getting to know students individually, so they feel comfortable.

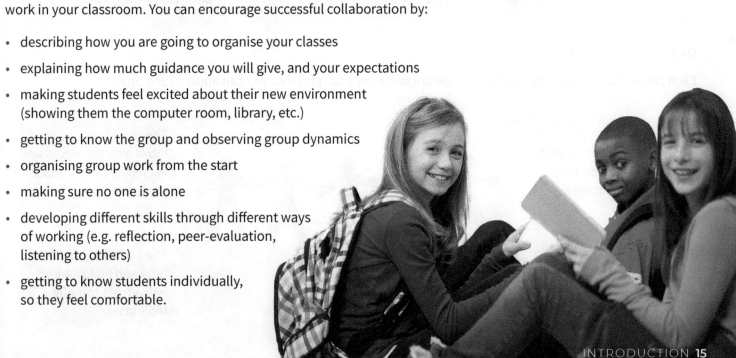

COLLABORATION

Collaborative skills	Behaviours	Level 1 Projects
Peer-tutoring	Correcting and editing each other's work	**A poster:** check spelling, grammar and punctuation of different group members
Resolving conflicts	Reaching a compromise and making final decisions	**A class survey:** suggest alternatives for presenting results; have a vote; listen to all opinions
Listening actively	Responding to others' work or suggestions	**A haiku:** give opinions on poems; reflect on outcome; suggest improvements
Giving positive feedback	Commenting on group members' work	**A food truck:** say what you like about the design, and what is creative or original
Encouraging responsibility	Completing tasks on time to finish a project together	**A lookbook:** bring examples to class; complete a page or section; check, edit and finalise
Using social skills	Giving opinions, persuading, compromising, agreeing	**An information leaflet:** decide what to include; give reasons for choices
Disagreeing appropriately	Giving opinions politely to come to a solution	**A scrapbook:** say why you don't like something and suggest ways to improve it; accept others' suggestions and make a decision together
Sharing resources	Helping group members to complete or improve work	**An interview:** lend or borrow recording equipment
Sharing tasks	Checking all group members have a role Choosing and working on tasks	**A webpage:** give sections to different members; create roles (illustrator, writer, designer, editor etc.)

Roles and responsibilities

Each project has specific roles, however here are some general roles that you can apply at any time.

The **group leader** supervises, communicates with the teacher and manages participation.

The **resource manager** looks after resources and keeps the final product for presentation.

The **diary keeper** records decisions and tracks roles and responsibilities.

The **coordinator** tracks time and makes sure individuals complete their tasks.

The **inspector** checks and edits information.

The flipped classroom

Project work and the flipped classroom

During

Put together work, edit, share opinions, present, give feedback, peer-evaluate

LEARNING OUTCOMES → LEARNING OUTCOMES → LEARNING OUTCOMES →

Before

Research, interview, prepare reports, make illustrations, organise sentences

After

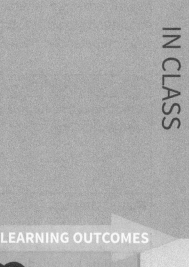

Complete learning diaries, reflect, self-evaluate

Each project in this book contains at least one flipped classroom idea. Students are still collaborating when they use this approach. They have to share roles, get things ready on time, share information and resources and check one another's work. Students should plan out-of-class project work and use their My time-management plans. **> My time-management plan p71**

How well did I collaborate?

At the end of the process, have students answer a few questions about how well they collaborated.

Did I ...
help my group?
share information?
do the tasks for my role?

Was I motivated?

Did we ...
trust each other in my group?
share opinions in my group?
share materials in my group?

What can I do to be a better group member?

PRESENTATION IDEAS

The end goal of project work is the presentation step. This is when students are able to show their final product and how they have achieved their learning outcomes.

As well as being a natural way to end the project process, this stage also gives you an opportunity to assess students' progress in the foundational layers of the Cambridge Life Competencies Framework. > Cambridge Life Competencies Framework p6

FOUNDATION LAYERS	ABILITIES	EXAMPLE ACTIONS
Emotional Development and Wellbeing	• Identify and understand emotions • Manage emotions • Empathise and build relationships	reflecting on strengths and weaknesses, verbalising emotions, employing coping mechanisms, adapting to stressful emotions, caring for others
Digital Literacy	• Use digital tools	creating documents, collaborating, sharing work, finding content, following safe practices
Discipline Knowledge	• Convince the audience	giving details, using facts and logic, demonstrating knowledge, summarising information, answering questions

Here are a few practical considerations when facilitating the presentation stage.

✓ Allow students enough time to prepare.

✓ Ensure students support each other – particularly shy students – before, during and after the presentation.

✓ Remind students of the learning outcomes and *why* they are presenting.

✓ Give students a reason for listening to presentations (peer-evaluation) and leave time for questions and discussion.

The following page gives ideas for ways to present some of the Level 1 projects. However, they are only suggestions. Where possible, let students choose modes of presentation that are most suitable for their projects and the classroom context.

1 Leaflets or brochures

Have students use word-processing programs to make leaflets and find websites for making digital posters online.

1. **Choose a format**
   (bi-fold or tri-fold)

2. **Choose a title**
   (brief and informative)

3. **Decide on sections**
   (information grouped together, space for images)

4. **Add text**
   (simple sentences)

5. **Add icons and images**
   (related to text)

6. **Check, correct and edit**
   (final version)

2 Posters

1. **Summarise** the poster in one short and concise title.

2. **Add** essential details that support the poster's main objective.

3. **Encourage** the reader to take the next step.

4. **Choose** appropriate fonts, and make sure there is a hierarchy for titles, subtitles and text.

5. **Use** relevant and interesting visuals.

6. **Emphasise** key features on different backgrounds.

3 Webpages

1. **Look at** an example of a **wireframe** (show students the elements of a webpage).

2. **Research** more examples of webpage designs and make sketches.

3. **Choose** a favourite webpage design and arrange the information into sections.

4. **Find** an online webpage template similar to the design chosen.

5. **Follow** the online steps to complete the product this way.

Wireframe

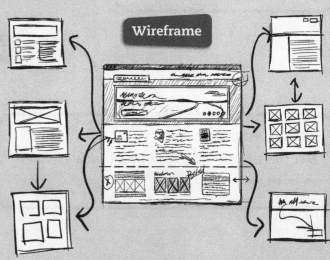

EVALUATION

What?

Product

How well did students achieve their **learning outcomes**?

How well did they demonstrate these?

How did they **evaluate options** and make **decisions**?

Process

How well did students **plan** the product?

How well did students **develop** the project (roles and responsibilities, research and analysis)?

Did students develop **life competencies**?

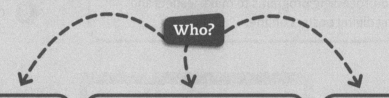

Who?

| Self-evaluation | Peer-evaluation | Teacher–student evaluation |

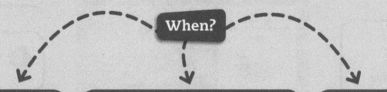

When?

Preparation

After groups are formed: checking learning outcomes, brainstorming ideas, identifying key information, making decisions about content

Development

After each step: thinking about roles and responsibilities, researching and analysing findings, drafting and reviewing

Production

Before presentation: deciding on how to present

During presentation: practising presentation skills

After: giving feedback and self-evaluating

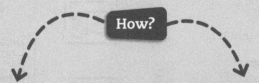

How?

Informal evaluation tools

KWL chart, My learning diary, Peer-evaluation form

> Evaluation tools pp67–69

Formal evaluation tools

Project evaluation rubrics, evaluation rubric, teacher's evaluation form

> Evaluation rubric p21

> Teacher's evaluation form p70

EVALUATION RUBRIC

The rubric below covers areas you can evaluate in every project. You can select some or all of these for each project when you feel it is necessary. There are also two project-specific rubrics with adapted evaluation descriptors in each unit.

Exceeds expectations (4): students show they are ready to go further and can take extra challenges in certain areas.

Very good (3): students complete the tasks successfully and as expected.

Good (2): students complete the tasks reasonably well with some things done better than others.

Needs improvement (1): students show room for improvement in most areas evaluated.

	4	3	2	1
Learning outcomes	Completes all stages to successfully achieve the overall learning outcomes.	Completes most stages effectively. Largely achieves overall learning outcomes.	Has missed some stages. Partially completes overall learning outcomes.	Hasn't successfully completed any of the stages. Overall learning outcomes unachieved.
Planning and organisation	Product is well organised, interesting and easy to follow. It follows the model for the project and no details are missing.	Product is well organised and easy to follow. Some details are incorrect or missing.	Product is similar to the model for the project, but is missing important information. It follows the model with difficulty.	Product does not look or sound anything like the one specified in the task. There is little or no sequence to ideas.
Use of information and resources	Uses a wide range of resources to get information about the product.	Uses different resources to get information, with some gaps.	Most information is relevant and useful, but only comes from one or two resources.	There is little evidence of research and hasn't used appropriate resources.
Collaboration (Teamwork)	Collaborated in all stages and understood roles and responsibilities.	Collaborated in all stages and understood responsibilities. There was minor confusion about roles and responsibilities.	Collaborated in most stages but there was some confusion about roles and responsibilities.	There was little or no collaboration throughout all stages. Didn't recognise roles and responsibilities.
Time management	Completed everything on time. Revised and corrected project.	Completed everything on time, with one or two steps at the last minute. Revised and corrected project.	Completed all steps, but at the last minute. There was little time for revision or correction.	Did not finish project. Missed steps in the process.
Creativity	Product is very original and interesting. All ideas are well developed.	Product is interesting and very creative. Most ideas are well developed.	There is some evidence of creativity which could have been developed. Product is a mixture of original and copied ideas.	Little creativity. Most ideas copied and pasted from other sources.
Problem-solving skills	All group members participate and listen actively to solve problems at all times.	Most group members are actively involved to solve most problems.	Some evidence of problem-solving but not by all group members.	Little or no evidence of problem-solving, either individually or in groups.
Language use	Excellent use of language. Project is clear and understandable with only a few mistakes.	Good use of language. Project is clear and understandable with some mistakes.	Adequate use of language. Project is understandable, but some sections need further explanation.	Random words are used in a confusing way. Project is almost impossible to understand.
Presentation skills	All group members participate. Presentation is well put-together and is clear and interesting throughout.	All group members participate. Presentation is mostly clear and interesting.	All group members participate, but the method of presentation is sometimes inappropriate or not engaging.	None of the group members fully participate. Inappropriate and uninteresting method of presentation.
Final product	Extremely good.	Very good.	Good.	Needs improvement.

A POSTER

- **Learning outcome:** design a poster

- **Skills:** research and select facts and visuals about a festival, make a spidergram to organise information, correct and edit each other's work

- **Resources:** two or more posters, Poster organiser p58, My time-management plan p71

- **Evaluation tools:** Project evaluation rubric p25, My learning diary p68, Peer-evaluation form p69, Teacher's evaluation form p70

 Unit 1

Before you start

Collect two or three different posters about events to show students in class.

1 Preparation

Step 1: Introduce the topic

- Introduce the topic of posters after doing the reading exercises.  Unit 1

- Show students the posters. Encourage them to say what they are for and where we can find them. Ask: *Are these events interesting? Why / Why not?*

- Explain that posters use text and pictures to get people's attention. Ask: *What kind of information is on posters? (Information about festivals, shows, movies, concerts, etc.)*

- Ask students to bring a poster to the next class (in their own language or English). They can discuss which posters they like and why.

☉ Flipped classroom activities

Step 2: Analyse the model for the project Unit 1

Out of class: have students read the model poster and answer the questions: *What is the important information? What is interesting? Do you like the pictures? Is this a festival for you?*

In class: have students discuss their ideas.

Ask students to compare the model poster with the examples they brought to class.

🛡 Creative Thinking
Creating new content from own ideas or other resources

Monitor students' ideas during the class discussion in Step 2 and write the best ones on the board. Then tell students to choose three ideas they'd like to use in their poster.

Step 3: *How to* design a poster Unit 1

- Go through the *How to* tips with the class. Explain that organising information well makes for a good poster. Say that a short and clear title is better than a long one. Point out that neat handwriting and well-written information also help the reader. Finally, discuss where students can find images and give them the option of presenting their posters digitally.

- Check students understand that, when they design their posters, they should use the ideas in this *How to* section.

Step 4: Clarify the project 🖱 Unit 1

- Follow the steps in **> The learning stages of project work p10**

- Brainstorm different festivals. Write a list on the board, together with any information students already know.

- Have groups choose a festival for their poster.

- If groups are thinking of presenting digitally, tell them to find programs they can use easily.

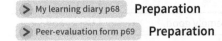

> My learning diary p68   **Preparation**

> Peer-evaluation form p69   **Preparation**

② Development

Start this stage as soon as groups know their learning outcomes and have chosen a festival for their poster.

Step 1: Assign roles and responsibilities

- In project groups, have students give each other general roles. **> Roles and responsibilities p16** Help them decide on further roles they can share, such as the ones in the diagram.

Step 2: Research and analyse ⏱ p71

- Hand out a copy of the **> Poster organiser p58** to each student. In their groups, students decide which section(s) each one will research.

⟳ **Flipped classroom activity**

Out of class: group members find information for their section(s) and write notes in their organiser.

Step 3: Draft and review ➤ Unit 1 ⏱ p71

In class: have groups do some of the P L A N section from **Exercise 1**. They put together the information from their organisers by making a group spidergram. Then they agree on who will draft each section – we suggest each member prepares the part they were assigned in Step 2.

Out of class: group members draft their section(s).

In class: group members check each other's sections and put their poster together. Allow time for final reviewing.

🛡 Collaboration
Managing the sharing of tasks in a project
Monitor progress of the tasks in Steps 2 and 3. Check that group members are looking at each other's work, making suggestions and actively participating. (See Differentiated instruction activities opposite for further practice.)

The **writer** produces the text and suggests titles.

The **proofreader** checks grammar, punctuation and spelling.

The **designer** arranges the images.

The **illustrator** suggests borders, fonts and colours.

The **picture manager** helps choose the images.

Differentiated instruction

Support
Help students self- and peer-correct their sections. Encourage suggestions for improvements.

Consolidation
Encourage students to use different sources (websites, dictionaries, their Student's Book) to check grammar, vocabulary and spelling.

Extension
Have students make final decisions over corrections, and explain their arguments to their group.

> My learning diary p68 **Development**
> Peer-evaluation form p69 **Development**

3 Production

Schedule presentation times and stick to them, asking all groups to present their posters. Spread the presentations over a few classes, if necessary. Allow enough time for each presentation and for questions.

Before groups produce their final drafts, ask them how they will present their posters (print or digital) and give ideas.

> Presentation ideas p18

As students complete their projects, check their abilities in the following Areas of Competency.

Creative Thinking
Creating new content from own ideas or other resources

Illustrates a new poster with unique symbols or persuasive language.
Evidence: Poster has a title, clear information and interesting visuals.

Responds imaginatively to contemporary events and ideas.
Evidence: Students transfer the notes from their spidergram to their poster in an attractive way.

Collaboration
Managing the sharing of tasks in a project

Works with others to plan and execute class projects.
Evidence: Group members complete their tasks with help from each other.

Ensures that all members have a role in group activities.
Evidence: Group members divide the work and share information.

Step 1: Prepare 🔺 Unit 1 ⏰ p71

- Go through the checklist in the PRESENT section in **Exercise 2**.

- As groups prepare their project, ask questions: *Does your poster have photos, maps and drawings? Is the title short and interesting? Is this word/sentence correct? Are these facts correct?* Allow enough time for final changes. Encourage groups to practise and time their presentation.

- Remind groups of the presentation date and how much time each group will have.

🔔 *Own it!* learning tip

Peer-tutoring

Monitor group members as they correct and edit each other's work. Explain that this includes checking grammar, punctuation and spelling. Encourage students to use dictionaries, such as the Cambridge Dictionary: **https://dictionary.cambridge.org/**. Have them use grammar references and help them with above-level structures. Have students refer to the model poster for punctuation such as question marks, exclamation marks and colons.

Step 2: Present 🔺 Unit 1

- Draw attention to the CHECK section from **Exercise 3**. Ask the class to think about these questions as they listen to each other's presentations.

- If the poster is digital, we suggest one group member is chosen as the technician. Have each group choose their technician.

- Have groups present their posters. If some students find it difficult to speak in front of the class, tell them to take their time and breathe deeply. Allow group members to help each other.

- Remind speakers to interact with their audience and ask for questions at the end of their presentation.

Step 3: Reflect 🔺 Unit 1

- After the presentations, hold a class discussion on the CHECK questions in **Exercise 3**.

  - Discuss different steps of the project process and the final result. Ask: *Are you happy with your poster? Which section is your favourite? Why? Is planning/researching/designing a poster easy/difficult? Why / Why not?*

> Peer-evaluation form p69   **Production**

🔺 Go to the digital collaboration space to set, track and assess students' work, or allow students to share and comment on their own work.

Project evaluation rubric: a poster

Use these project-specific descriptors and your own choice of descriptors from the > Evaluation rubric p21 to check students individually or in groups. Make your own evaluation form. > Teacher's evaluation form p70

	4	3	2	1
Creativity	Product is well organised with creative and interesting ideas. It has a short and interesting title and important information. It includes interesting borders, photos, maps and drawings.	Product is organised with interesting ideas. It has a short and interesting title and most of the important information. It includes borders, photos, maps and drawings.	Product has interesting ideas but lacks organisation. It has a title and some important information. It includes photos, maps and drawings, but the borders and design are not attractive.	Product lacks interesting ideas and organisation. It is missing a title and/or important information. It doesn't include any design features and the visuals are not related to the topic.
Language use	Shows excellent use of grammar, punctuation and spelling. Project is understandable with only a few mistakes.	Product shows good use of grammar, punctuation and spelling. Project is understandable with some mistakes.	Product shows adequate use of grammar, punctuation and spelling. Project is understandable, but some sections need further explanation.	Product shows poor use of grammar, punctuation and spelling. Project is confusing and almost impossible to understand.

 Cambridge Life Competencies Framework
You can also check students' progress in the following foundation layers.

FOUNDATION LAYERS	ABILITIES	ACTIONS
Digital Literacy	• Use digital tools	finding content on various websites, cross-checking facts with other digital sources, using digital tools to design and present posters
Emotional Development and Wellbeing	• Empathise and build relationships	reflecting on strengths and weaknesses, helping others complete their tasks, using coping mechanisms when giving presentations (such as taking some time and breathing deeply)

Flipped classroom activities

Evaluate

In project groups, have students discuss their completed Peer-evaluation forms and ways to work better as a group. > Peer-evaluation form p69

Out of class: have students reflect on their progress at home. > My learning diary p68 **Production**

In class: hold a class discussion on what students learned using the information from their learning diaries. > My learning diary p68 **Production**

A CLASS SURVEY

- **Learning outcome:** do a class survey

- **Skills:** ask questions and record information, draw a bar chart, present and give opinions on survey results

- **Resources:** two or more surveys, Class survey organiser p59, My time-management plan p71

- **Evaluation tools:** Project evaluation rubric p29, KWL chart p67, Peer-evaluation form p69, Teacher's evaluation form p70

 Student's Book pp30–31

Before you start
Collect two or three different surveys from magazines or the internet to show students in class.

Preparation

Step 1: Introduce the topic

- Introduce the topic of surveys after doing the street interviews listening exercises. 📖 p26

- Explain that surveys use questions to find out information from a number of people. You ask the questions, record the answers and present the results in graphs or charts. You can then draw conclusions. Ask students if they know of any surveys and what the results are.

- Show students the surveys. Encourage them to say what they are and what their purpose is. Ask: *Who does surveys and why? What are these surveys about?*

- Ask students to bring a survey to the next class (these don't need to be in English). They can discuss which results are interesting and why.

Step 2: Analyse the model for the project 📖 pp30–31

- 🎧 2.12 Complete Exercises 1 to 3. Play the audio for **Exercise 2**. Check answers.

  Answers **1** b **2** 1 9 2 23 3 7 4 12 5 20 6 3 7 0 **3** 2 What the students in their class do on Saturday mornings. **3** In a bar chart. **4** Playing video games.

- Ask questions about the effectiveness of the survey, for example: *Is the purpose clear? What is the topic question? How many students take part in the survey? Can you understand the bar chart?*

- Revise the language from the unit. Ask students to find examples of the present simple.

Step 3: *How to* present survey results 📖 p30

- 🎧 2.13 Students do **Exercise 4**. Play the audio to check answers.

  Answers **4** 2 students **3** girls **4** question **5** results **6** surprising **7** class

- Go through the *How to* tips in **Exercise 5** with the class. Have students find examples of the tips in the model survey.

- 🎧 2.13 Play the audio for **Exercise 5**. Students check their answers and share their opinions in pairs or groups. Then ask: *What do you think of the conclusion?*

  Answers **5** 1 Yes. 2 The results are interesting: most of the students play video games, only three students stay in bed late and no one tidies their bedroom on Saturday morning. 3 Students' own answer

- Ensure students understand that, when they present their survey results, they should use the tips in this *How to* section.

Critical Thinking
Evaluating ideas, arguments and options
Use the questions in Steps 2 and 3 to check how well students understand the purpose, results and conclusions of the survey, and what reasons they give for their arguments.

Step 4: Clarify the project 📖 pp30–31

- Follow the steps in  The learning stages of project work p10 .

- Brainstorm the main parts of a survey: topic question and purpose, number of people, questions, summary of results and conclusions.

- Have groups choose one of the topics from the P L A N section, **Exercise 6**. If there are more than four groups, give additional ideas, such as 📖 Student's Book pp30–31 and *Indoor vs. outdoor activities*. Tell groups to decide on the purpose of their survey and think of a topic question.

> KWL chart p67   **Know and Want to know**

> Peer-evaluation form p69   **Preparation**

② Development

Start this stage as soon as groups know their learning outcomes and have thought of their topic question.

Step 1: Assign roles and responsibilities

- In project groups, have students decide on general roles. > Roles and responsibilities p16   Help them decide on further roles they can share, such as the ones in the diagram.

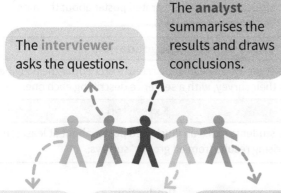

The **analyst** summarises the results and draws conclusions.

The **interviewer** asks the questions.

The **researcher** helps choose the activities to include.

The **note-taker** makes notes of the answers.

The **statistician** adds up the results and presents them in a bar chart.

🛡 Communication
Using appropriate language and register for context

Monitor progress of the tasks in Step 3 to check that groups summarise their results in a clear way. Focus on the use of the present simple and presentation of information.

Step 2: Research and analyse 📖 p31 ⏰ p71

- Have groups complete the rest of the P L A N section from **Exercise 6**. Remind them to write their topic question.

- Groups brainstorm activities related to their topic question and choose six for their survey. They then write the questions.

- Allow enough class time for groups to conduct their surveys in a way that works for your class. For example, have the interviewer and note-taker from one group come to the front. The interviewer reads their questions, and the class raise their hands to answer *yes* or *no*. The note-taker counts and records the number. Repeat with all questions and all groups.

- Groups analyse their results and draw conclusions.

- Hand out a copy of the > Class survey organiser p59 to each student.

🔄 Flipped classroom activity

Step 3: Draft and review 📖 p31 ⏰ p71

Out of class: have students complete their organisers and bring them to the next class.

In class: have groups draft a final survey using ideas from their organisers. Encourage discussion about how to present the results and what conclusions to make.

Check that group members help prepare each part in accordance with their roles.

♻ *Own it!* learning tip

Resolving conflicts

If group members don't agree on how to present the results or on the conclusions, encourage them to reach a compromise and make a final decision. Ask them to suggest alternatives, have a vote and listen to everyone's opinions. Monitor to help with useful language, for example: *Why don't we say … , Let's write … , We can try …*

> Peer-evaluation form p69   **Preparation**

③ Production

Schedule presentation times and stick to them, so that all groups can present their surveys. Spread the presentations over a few classes, if necessary. Allow enough time for each presentation and for questions.

Before groups produce their final drafts, have them decide on the format for their survey. They could present their bar chart digitally or as a poster. > Presentation ideas p18

As students complete their projects, check their abilities in the following Areas of Competency.

 Communication

Using appropriate language and register for context

Knows how to present points clearly and persuasively.
Evidence: Results are presented correctly as a bar chart and they lead to clear conclusions.

Uses language for effect (exaggerations).
Evidence: Attention is drawn to surprising or interesting results.

 Critical Thinking

Evaluating ideas, arguments and options

Identifies evidence and its reliability.
Evidence: Students draw logical conclusions from their survey results.

Gives reasons for an argument's plausibility.
Evidence: Students explain surprising or interesting results.

Step 1: Prepare 📖 p31 ⏰ p71

- Go through the checklist in the PRESENT section from **Exercise 7**.

- As groups prepare their project, ask questions, for example: *Is the bar chart accurate? Is the summary of the results correct? Do you agree on the conclusions?*

- Check use of the present simple. Allow enough time for final adjustments.

- Remind groups of the presentation date and how much time each group will have.

Step 2: Present 📖 p31

- For this project, we suggest every group member presents their part of the survey, with the main parts being the purpose, the topic question and activities, the bar chart, the results and the conclusions.

- Draw attention to the CHECK section from **Exercise 8**. Ask the class to do the task as they listen to each other presentations.

- Have groups present their surveys.

- Remind groups to give their audience time to study the bar chart and results.

Step 3: Reflect 📖 p31

- After the presentations, have the class share their ideas from the CHECK section in **Exercise 8**. Encourage students to give positive feedback on interesting or surprising results.

- Grade activities for the Present and Check steps, if necessary. (See Differentiated instruction activities below for further practice.)

Differentiated instruction

Support
Have students make an illustrated poster about the most popular activities in the class.

Consolidation
Have students make an illustrated poster about the activities from their survey, with a sentence describing each one.

Extension
Have students make an illustrated poster about at least four surprising results from all groups' surveys.

> Peer-evaluation form p69 **Production**

 Go to the digital collaboration space to set, track and assess students' work, or allow students to share and comment on their own work.

Project evaluation rubric: a class survey

Use these project-specific descriptors and your own choice of descriptors from the > Evaluation rubric p21 to check students individually or in groups. Make your own evaluation form. > Teacher's evaluation form p70

	4	3	2	1
Creativity	Product is well organised and includes surprising or interesting results. It uses a very clear bar chart. It shows a purpose and an interesting topic question. It draws interesting conclusions.	Product is organised and includes surprising or interesting results. It uses a clear bar chart. It shows a purpose and a topic question. It draws conclusions.	Product is fairly well organised and presents results, but does not focus on anything interesting or surprising. It uses a bar chart with some mistakes. It shows a purpose and a topic question, but they are not fully related. It draws conclusions, but some are inaccurate.	Product is poorly organised and the results are confusing. It uses a bar chart, but it is not clear. It does not show a purpose or a topic question. It draws inaccurate conclusions.
Language use	Excellent use of language from unit (present simple). Project is understandable with only a few mistakes.	Good use of language from unit (present simple). Project is understandable with some mistakes.	Adequate use of language from unit (present simple). Project is understandable, but some sections need further explanation.	Poor or no use of language from unit (present simple). Project is confusing and almost impossible to understand.

 Cambridge Life Competencies Framework
You can also check students' progress in the following foundation layers.

FOUNDATION LAYERS	ABILITIES	ACTIONS
Emotional Development and Wellbeing	• Manage emotions	verbalising emotions appropriately when resolving conflicts, making compromises as a group
Discipline Knowledge	• Convince the audience	explaining facts and images, giving details, summarising information, drawing conclusions

○ Flipped classroom activities

Evaluate

In project groups, have students discuss their completed Peer-evaluation forms and ways to work better as a group. > Peer-evaluation form p69

Out of class: have students reflect on their progress at home. > KWL chart p67 **Learned**

In class: hold a class discussion on what students know now, using the information from their KWL charts.
> KWL chart p67 **Learned**

A HAIKU

- **Learning outcome:** write a haiku
- **Skills:** brainstorm words related to the haiku topic, organise words into sentences, speak to a large group
- **Resources:** two or more haikus, Haiku organiser p60, My time-management plan p71
- **Evaluation tools:** Project evaluation rubric p33, My learning diary p68, Peer-evaluation form p69, Teacher's evaluation form p70

 Unit 3

Before you start

Collect two or three different haikus to show students in class.

1 Preparation

Step 1: Introduce the topic

- Introduce the topic of haikus after doing the Learn to Learn exercise. 📖 p38 Ask: *What is a haiku? Where are they from?* Then read the haiku definition Unit 3 to check students' answers.

- Show students the haikus on a screen or write them on the board. Read them aloud and count the number of lines and syllables with the class. Go over the structure again.

- Explain that haikus can be about any topic and that they always follow the same structure. Say that they don't rhyme. Ask what the example haikus are about.

- Ask students to bring a haiku to the next class (in their own language or English). They can say what they are about.

Step 2: Analyse the model for the project 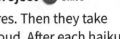 Unit 3

- Have students describe the pictures. Then they take turns to read the model haikus aloud. After each haiku, ask: *What is the topic?*

- Ask more questions about the haikus, for example: *Do they follow the correct structure? Which one is your favourite? Why?*

Step 3: *How to* **speak to a large group** Unit 3

- Go through the *How to* tips with the class. Then tell students that you will read one of the model haikus aloud, following some of the tips but not others. When you have finished, read out each tip again. Students tell you which ones you followed.

- Check students understand that, when they present their haikus, they should use the ideas in this *How to* section.

> 🛡️ **Social Responsibilities**
> **Taking active roles including leadership**
>
> In groups, have students take turns to read the model haikus aloud. Tell them to follow the *How to* tips. Encourage students to choose one of the haikus and try to say it from memory.

Step 4: Clarify the project Unit 3

- Follow the steps in > The learning stages of project work p10 .

- Brainstorm different topics for haikus. Review the structure of a haiku (the number of lines and syllables per line).

- Tell students that they will each write their own haiku on a topic of their choice. Then they will check each other's work in their project groups.

> My learning diary p68   **Preparation**

> Peer-evaluation form p69   **Preparation**

2 Development

Start this stage as soon as groups know their learning outcomes and have brainstormed ideas for haikus.

Step 1: Assign roles and responsibilities

- In project groups, have students decide on general roles. **> Roles and responsibilities p16** Help them decide on further roles they can share, such as those in the diagram.

The **camera operator** films people practising their haikus.

The **proofreader** checks spelling, grammar and vocabulary.

The **editor** checks the number of lines and syllables.

The **voice coach** checks the speed and clarity of people's speech.

The **adviser** checks eye contact, body posture and facial expressions.

Step 2: Research and analyse Unit 3 p71

- Tell students first to work on their own. Have them start the PLAN section from **Exercise 1** and choose a topic for their haiku. They can use the ideas in the box, the brainstormed ideas, or their own.

- Hand out a copy of the **> Haiku organiser p60** to each student. Have them make notes about how they feel and draw or find some pictures.

- Tell students to complete the second part of their organisers (the spidergram) on their own. Then encourage group members to help brainstorm more topic words to add to each one's spidergrams.

⟳ Flipped classroom activities

Step 3: Draft and review Unit 3 p71

Out of class: have students complete the PLAN section, using their organisers. Encourage them to use their imagination and creativity. Suggest they choose their favourite words, write sentences and count the number of syllables in each line. Say that they may need to change words if their lines don't have the correct number of syllables.

In class: group members check each other's haikus, with editors and proofreaders taking leading roles.

Each student writes their final haiku. Grade activities for this step, if necessary. (See Differentiated instruction activities below for further practice.)

Differentiated instruction

Support
Tell students which words need changing and how many syllables their new words need.
Consolidation
Encourage students to use dictionaries to find synonyms and other topic-related words for their haiku.
Extension
Have students use their words to write different versions of their haiku and decide on the best one with their group members.

⛉ Learning to Learn
Practical skills for participating in learning

Check students' notes and final haikus when they complete Step 3. Check that they use sentences that fit the haiku structure.

> My learning diary p68 Development

> Peer-evaluation form p69 Development

③ Production

Schedule presentation times and stick to them, checking that everyone presents their haikus. You could aim for all students reading their haikus in just one class.

You can also ask students to write their final haikus as illustrated posters. These can be individual or group posters. Point to the model haiku. 🖱 Unit 3

> Presentation ideas p18

As students complete their projects, check their abilities in the following Areas of Competency.

🛡 Social Responsibilities
Taking active roles including leadership

Check students' notes and final haiku when they complete Step 3. Check that they use sentences that fit the haiku structure.

Sets strategies and plans.

Evidence: Students follow the ideas in the *How to* section and use them to give feedback.

Shows confidence in speaking in public (e.g. to present a project).

Evidence: Students read their haikus clearly and confidently to the class.

🛡 Learning to Learn
Practical skills for participating in learning

Organises notes systematically.

Evidence: Students use the notes in their Haiku organisers to structure their haikus.

Uses notes to construct original output.

Evidence: Students present original haikus with topic-related vocabulary.

🔈 *Own it!* learning tip

Listening actively

Although each group member has a specific role, encourage all members to listen to each other's haikus and give feedback. Have them use the ideas in the *How to* section to give advice on body posture and eye contact, and to remember to smile and speak clearly. Encourage students to use language from the unit, such as: *I like/love … . I can't hear you. You can read well!*

Step 1: Prepare 🖱 Unit 3 ⏰ p71

- Go through the checklist in the PRESENT section from **Exercise 2**.

- As students prepare their haikus, ask questions, for example: *Does your haiku have the correct number of lines/syllables? Does it show your feelings?*

- Have students practise presenting their haikus in their groups. Remind them to use the ideas in the *How to* section.

Step 2: Present 🖱 Unit 3

- Draw attention to the CHECK section from **Exercise 3**. Ask the class to think about these questions as they listen to their peers' presentations.

- Tell students to remember the ideas in the *How to* section when they speak.

- Have students present their haikus.

- If groups made posters, display them around the room.

Step 3: Reflect 🖱 Unit 3

- After the presentations, hold a class discussion on the CHECK questions in **Exercise 3**.

- Discuss the haikus. Ask: *What are the haikus about? Which is your favourite? Why?*

- Encourage students to think about each stage of the project process, including positive experiences and things they could improve.

> Peer-evaluation form p69   **Production**

🖱 Go to the digital collaboration space to set, track and assess students' work, or allow students to share and comment on their own work.

Project evaluation rubric: a haiku

Use these project-specific descriptors and your own choice of descriptors from the > Evaluation rubric p21 to check students individually or in groups. Make your own evaluation form. > Teacher's evaluation form p70

	4	3	2	1
Creativity	Product is very well written with a clear topic and related vocabulary. It follows the haiku structure and is easy to understand. It uses language in an imaginative way.	Product is well written with a fairly clear topic and related vocabulary. It is one or two syllables away from the haiku structure, but is easy to understand. It uses language in a fairly imaginative way.	Product is adequately written with appropriate vocabulary, but the topic is not very clear. One or two of its lines follow the haiku structure and it is fairly understandable. It uses appropriate language, but not in an imaginative way.	Product is poorly written with an unclear topic and unrelated vocabulary. It doesn't follow the haiku structure and it is difficult to understand. It doesn't use language in an imaginative way.
Presentation skills	Speaks slowly, clearly and confidently. Looks at the audience and smiles. Keeps very good time.	Speaks slowly, clearly and confidently most of the time. Looks at the audience and smiles most of the time. Keeps good time.	Speaks slowly, clearly and confidently some of the time. Looks at the audience and smiles some of the time. Is slightly too slow or fast.	Doesn't speak clearly or confidently. Doesn't look at the audience or smile. Is much too slow or fast.

 Cambridge Life Competencies Framework
You can also check students' progress in the following foundation layers.

FOUNDATION LAYERS	ABILITIES	ACTIONS
Discipline Knowledge	• Convince the audience	conveying a clear message, using appropriate vocabulary, following the structure of a haiku
Emotional Development and Wellbeing	• Manage emotions	adapting to stressful situations (speaking in front of a large group) by using coping mechanisms (such as taking a deep breath and speaking slowly), caring for others (giving positive feedback)

↻ Flipped classroom activities

Evaluate

In project groups, have students discuss their completed Peer-evaluation forms and ways to work better as a group. > Peer-evaluation form p69

Out of class: have students reflect on their progress at home. > My learning diary p68 **Production**

In class: hold a class discussion on what students know now, using the information from their learning diaries. > My learning diary p68 **Production**

A FOOD TRUCK

- **Learning outcome:** design a food truck
- **Skills:** decide and agree on a menu, create an attractive design, evaluate own and others' design projects
- **Resources:** two or more food truck images, A3 paper/card, Food truck organiser p61, My time-management plan p71
- **Evaluation tools:** Project evaluation rubric p37, KWL chart p67, Peer-evaluation form p69, Teacher's evaluation form p70

📖 Student's Book pp54–55

Before you start
Print out two or three images of food trucks from the internet to show students in class.

1 Preparation

Step 1: Introduce the topic
- Introduce the topic of food trucks after doing the reading exercises. 📖 p48
- Explain that food trucks are like restaurants on wheels. Many food trucks sell fast food and they move around from place to place.
- Show students the food truck images. Ask: *What kinds of food do they sell? How do you know? Is the menu easy to read? Do you like the truck's design? Do you want to eat there? Why / Why not?*
- Ask students to bring images of food trucks to the next class. They can discuss the designs and menus, and say which their favourite truck is and why.

 **Collaboration**
Taking personal responsibility for own contributions
Monitor students' ability to analyse the model food truck and encourage them to explain their answers during the discussion in Step 2.

Step 2: Analyse the model for the project 📖 pp54–55
- Complete **Exercises 1 to 3**.

  Answers **1** Students' own answers **2 2** Fresh vegetable soup. **3** £5.00 **4** Hot bananas with chocolate and peanut butter balls. **5** Buy one delicious dish and get one free sweet treat! **3** Students' own answers

- Ask questions about the model food truck design and menu: *Does the truck have a good name? Are the menu and prices clear? Are the dishes easy to find? What pictures are on the truck? How do they relate to the name and menu?*
- Revise the language from the unit. Ask students to find food words on the menu and classify them into countable and uncountable.

Step 3: *How to* evaluate a design 📖 p54
- 🎧 4.11 Go through the list in **Exercise 4** with the class. Encourage students to explain their choices. Then play the audio to check answers.

  Answers **4 a** design **b** content

- Have students do **Exercise 5**. Ask them to compare their evaluations in pairs and give reasons for their scores. Remind them of their ideas from Step 2.
- Check students understand that, when they evaluate their food truck designs, they should use the ideas in this *How to* section.

Step 4: Clarify the project 📖 pp54–55
- Follow the steps in > The learning stages of project work p10 .
- Brainstorm different types of food and food trucks and possible dishes for their menus.
- Have groups choose a type of food and discuss where they can find more information for dishes and drinks to sell.

> KWL chart p67 **Know and Want to know**

> Peer-evaluation form p69 **Preparation**

① Development

Start this stage as soon as groups know their learning outcomes and have chosen the type of food to sell in their food truck.

Step 1: Assign roles and responsibilities

- In project groups, have students decide on general roles. **> Roles and responsibilities p16** Help them decide on further roles they can share, such as the ones in the diagram.

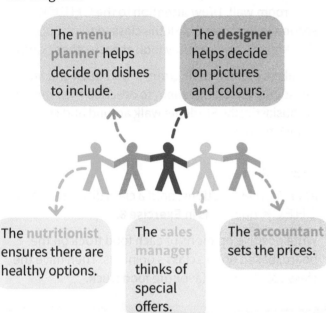

The **menu planner** helps decide on dishes to include.

The **designer** helps decide on pictures and colours.

The **nutritionist** ensures there are healthy options.

The **sales manager** thinks of special offers.

The **accountant** sets the prices.

Step 2: Research and analyse 📖 p55 ⏰ p71

- Hand out a copy of the **> Food truck organiser p61** to each student.

🔄 **Flipped classroom activities**

Out of class: have students go through the PLAN section from **Exercise 6** and complete their organiser with their ideas. Remind them to look for information in restaurants, cafés and the internet. Tell them to bring their notes to the next class.

In class: ask groups to go through each point in **Exercise 6** and compare their notes. Give each group one more Food truck organiser to complete with their best ideas.

- Check that students agree about the best ideas for completing their group organiser.
- Grade activities for this step, if necessary. (See Differentiated instruction activities above for further practice.)

Differentiated instruction

Support
Help students with language so they offer a variety of food, including main dishes, sweet food and special offers.
Consolidation
Help students with language for agreeing, disagreeing and making decisions, such as: *I think ... , In my opinion ... , We can/can't ... , Why don't we ...?*
Extension
Allow students to create two menus. Help them with ideas, such as vegetarian, economy or family menu.

🛡️ **Creative Thinking**
Using newly created content to solve problems

Monitor groups as they plan their food trucks and decide on titles, content and design.

Step 3: Draft and review 📖 p55 ⏰ p71

- Have students use the ideas from their group organiser to sketch a sign for their food truck.
- Group members suggest pictures and colours, with the designer taking the leading role.
- Encourage peer-correction and discussion about the best way to present the project.

> Peer-evaluation form p69 Development

3 Production

Schedule presentation times and stick to them, so that each group can present their food trucks. Spread the presentations over a few classes, if necessary. Allow enough time for each presentation and for questions.

Before groups produce their final drafts, have them decide on the format for presenting their food truck. You could suggest a poster, or a bi-fold or tri-fold leaflet.

> Presentation ideas p18

As students complete their projects, check their abilities in the following Areas of Competency.

Creative Thinking
Using newly created content to solve problems

Employs new ideas and content in solving a task or activity.

Evidence: There is creativity in content and design.

Makes an assignment original by adding new angles.

Evidence: Food truck includes special offers and options (vegetarian, healthy, etc.).

Collaboration
Taking personal responsibility for own contributions

Follows the instructions for a task.

Evidence: Steps for tasks are completed in a logical order and on time.

Explains reasons for their suggestions and contributions.

Evidence: All group members take part in making and explaining decisions.

Step 1: Prepare 📖 pp54–55 ⏱ p71

- Go through the checklist in the PRESENT section from **Exercise 7**.

- Hand out pieces of A3 paper/card as necessary. As groups prepare their projects, remind them of the tasks to complete. Ask: *Are there interesting dishes on the menu? Is the information clear? How can you make the design more attractive?* Tell them to use the table and key in **Exercise 5** to evaluate their own designs.

- Remind groups of the presentation date and how much time each group will have.

Step 2: Present 📖 p55

- For this project, we suggest each group chooses a speaker. Speakers will introduce their group members and present their food truck.

- Give speakers time to practise in front of their groups. Encourage groups to help their speakers with language from the unit, such as *there is* and *there are*, and with pronunciation.

- Have groups display their food trucks on the classroom wall. Draw attention to the CHECK section in **Exercise 8**. Ask the class to think about these instructions as they look at each other's designs.

- Speakers present their group's food truck and answer questions. Encourage them to describe their menus enthusiastically. Students walk around and check each other's designs.

Step 3: Reflect 📖 p55

- After the presentations, hold a class discussion on the CHECK questions in **Exercise 8**.

- Write positive opinions of each food truck on the board, based on the class's opinions. Then have the class vote for their favourite food truck.

🔄 *Own it!* learning tip

Giving positive feedback

As groups evaluate each other's designs, encourage them to say what they like about every project, and make suggestions for how something good can be better. Monitor to help with useful language, for example: *I like … , This is good because … , That is really clear … , I like it, but why don't you … ?*

> Peer-evaluation form p69   **Production**

🖱 Go to the digital collaboration space to set, track and assess students' work, or allow students to share and comment on their own work.

Project evaluation rubric: a food truck

Use these project-specific descriptors and your own choice of descriptors from the › Evaluation rubric p21 to think about students individually or in groups. Make your own evaluation form. › Teacher's evaluation form p70

	4	3	2	1
Creativity	Product has a very interesting and well-organised menu. It uses an attractive design with an imaginative title. It includes original pictures and colours. It gets a lot of positive feedback.	Product has an interesting and well-organised menu. It uses an attractive design with a relevant title. It includes appropriate pictures and colours. It gets mostly positive feedback.	Product has a standard and fairly organised menu. It uses an adequate design with a correct title. It includes some pictures and colours. It gets some positive feedback.	Product has an uninteresting and poorly organised menu. It doesn't use an adequate design and doesn't have a title. It includes very few or no pictures or colours. It doesn't get any positive feedback.
Language use	Product shows a wide range of food vocabulary. It is presented using the correct forms of *There is/There are* and countable and uncountable nouns.	Product shows a good range of food vocabulary. It is mostly presented using the correct forms of *There is/There are* and countable and uncountable nouns.	Product shows an adequate range of food vocabulary. It is presented occasionally using the correct forms of *There is/There are* and countable and uncountable nouns.	Product shows a poor range of food vocabulary. It is not presented using *There is/There are* or countable and uncountable nouns correctly.

Cambridge Life Competencies Framework

You can also check students' progress in the following foundation layers.

FOUNDATION LAYERS	ABILITIES	ACTIONS
Emotional Development and Wellbeing	• Empathise and build relationships	focusing and reflecting on the strengths of each other's projects, caring for others and giving positive feedback
Discipline Knowledge	• Convince the audience	explaining facts and images, demonstrating knowledge of types of food, giving details, answering questions

⟳ Flipped classroom activities

Evaluate

In project groups, have students discuss their completed Peer-evaluation forms and ways to work better as a group. › Peer-evaluation form p69

Out of class: have students think about their progress at home. › KWL chart p67 **Learned**

In class: hold a class discussion on what students know now, using the information from their KWL charts. › KWL chart p67 **Learned**

A LOOKBOOK

- **Learning outcome:** make a lookbook

- **Skills:** choose and research a style of clothes, find photos or draw pictures for it and describe them, present the lookbook

- **Resources:** two or more fashion catalogues, magazines or lookbooks; Lookbook organiser p62, My time-management plan p71

- **Evaluation tools:** Project evaluation rubric p41, My learning diary p68, Peer-evaluation form p69, Teacher's evaluation form p70

Unit5

Before you start

Collect two or three different fashion catalogues or magazines to show students in class. You can also show students some lookbook pages (online or in print).

1 Preparation

Step 1: Introduce the topic

- Introduce the topic of lookbooks after doing the reading exercises. p60 Ask: *What looks and styles does Michiko describe? Where can we see pictures or read about clothes and fashion?*

- Show students the catalogues and magazines. Ask: *What can you see in the photos? Why do people read these magazines? How are the pages similar or different?*

- Explain that lookbooks show and describe different styles of clothes. They usually show the latest fashions for a particular season. Ask: *How is a lookbook different from a catalogue? (A catalogue shows price, colour and size, but a lookbook only focuses on style.)*

- Ask students to find an example of a lookbook online to show in the next class (in their own language or English). They can describe the different styles of clothes.

Step 2: Analyse the model for the project 🖱 Unit 5

- Have students describe the pictures in the model lookbook. Then they read the text.

- Check comprehension. Ask: *Who is this style for? Where do people wear these clothes? What accessories can you see? Is the description positive or negative?*

- Draw attention to the design and purpose of the model lookbook. Ask: *Is the page attractive? Do you think this style is popular?*

Step 3: *How to* present a project 🖱 Unit 5

- Go through the *How to* tips with the class. Different students say why each idea is important.

- Check students understand that, when they present their lookbooks, they should use the ideas in this *How to* section.

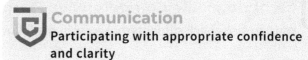
Communication
Participating with appropriate confidence and clarity

Ask: *Which 'How to present' ideas do you remember from past projects?* Then have students say which of the ideas are easy to follow, which ones are more difficult, and why.

Step 4: Clarify the project 🖱 Unit 5

- Follow the steps in > The learning stages of project work p10 .

- Brainstorm different styles of clothes and write a list on the board.

- Have groups discuss where they can find information about different styles of clothes. They can also think about who each style is for and how to present it (digitally or in print).

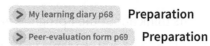
> My learning diary p68 **Preparation**

> Peer-evaluation form p69 **Preparation**

2 Development

Start this stage as soon as groups know their learning outcomes and have brainstormed styles of clothes to research.

Step 1: Assign roles and responsibilities

- In project groups, have students decide on the general roles. **> Roles and responsibilities p16** Help them decide on further roles they can share, such as those in the diagram.

The researcher helps find information about the style.

The digital editor manages the presentation of digital formats.

The fashion editor helps decide on images and information.

The picture manager helps find the images.

The designer arranges the images and text.

Step 2: Research and analyse 👆 Unit 5 ⏰ p71

- Have groups start the P L A N section from **Exercise 1** and choose a style of clothes.

- Hand out a copy of the **> Lookbook organiser p62** to each student. They make notes in the spidergram.

⟳ Flipped classroom activities

Out of class: have students finish their spidergrams. Encourage them to research their style on the internet or in fashion magazines. Tell them to look for photos to bring to the next class.

In class: have group members compare notes and put together a group spidergram.

Groups refer to their group spidergram and share their photos to plan their lookbook, using the Lookbook template in their organisers.

🛡 Learning to Learn
Taking control of your own learning

Encourage students to share resources with each other. Have them use dictionaries, such as the Cambridge Dictionary: **https://dictionary.cambridge.org/**, to find words for clothes and accessories, as well as fashion magazines and catalogues.

Step 3: Draft and review

- Have groups complete the rest of the P L A N section. When they have decided on a design for their lookbook, tell them to give each other sections to work on.

⟳ Flipped classroom activities

Out of class: students work on their section.

In class: have group members put their lookbook together. Allow them time to discuss and agree on final changes.

🏠 *Own it!* learning tip

Encouraging responsibility

Tell students it is important to complete their sections on time so that their groups can finish the project in class. Remind group members of their general roles. Discuss any problems groups may be having in keeping to schedule. Think about why this is happening and encourage or suggest possible solutions.

> **My learning diary p68** Development

> **Peer-evaluation form p69** Development

③ Production

Schedule presentation times and stick to them, so each group can present their lookbooks. Spread the presentations over a few classes, if necessary. Allow enough time for each presentation and for questions.

Some groups may choose to present their project digitally, for example, as a webpage. Have them use a webpage template. **> Presentation ideas p18**

As students complete their projects, check their abilities in the following Areas of Competency.

 Communication
Participating with appropriate confidence and clarity

Speaks with suitable fluency.

Evidence: **Students present without reading from their notes.**

Uses facial expressions and eye contact appropriately.

Evidence: **Students look at their audience and smile while presenting.**

 Learning to Learn
Taking control of your own learning

Identifies helpful resources for their learning.

Evidence: **Presentation has relevant information from a variety of sources.**

Uses a learner's dictionary and other reference resources.

Evidence: **Clothes and accessories are described and spelt correctly.**

Step 1: Prepare 🖱 Unit 5 ⏱ p71

- Go through the checklist in the PRESENT section in **Exercise 2**.

- As students prepare their sections, ask questions, for example: *Are you describing what people are wearing? Are there clothes and accessories? Are you checking each other's work?*

- Have students practise presenting their sections in their groups, using the ideas in the *How to* section.

- Grade activities for this step, if necessary. (See Differentiated instruction activities below for further practice.)

Differentiated instruction

Support
Check students' sections, highlighting problems with vocabulary and the use of present tenses. Encourage self-correction.
Consolidation
Check students' sections and suggest including more examples of the present simple or continuous.
Extension
Have group members check each other's sections. Tell them to pay attention to clothes vocabulary and the use of present tenses. Can they add anything new to each section?

Step 2: Present 🖱 Unit 5

- Draw attention to the CHECK section from **Exercise 3**. Ask the class to think about these questions as they listen to each other's presentations.

- Have groups present their lookbooks. Check that each member takes part in the presentation. Tell the class to make notes on what they like about each lookbook.

Step 3: Reflect 🖱 Unit 5

- After all the presentations, hold a class discussion on the CHECK questions in **Exercise 3**.

- Have the class say what they like about each lookbook and why, before holding a vote on their favourite.

- Encourage students to reflect on each stage of the project process, including positive experiences and things they could improve.

> Peer-evaluation form p69 **Production**

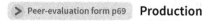 Go to the digital collaboration space to set, track and assess students' work, or allow students to share and comment on their own work.

Project evaluation rubric: a lookbook

Use these project-specific descriptors and your own choice of descriptors from the **> Evaluation rubric p21** to check students individually or in groups. Make your own evaluation form. **> Teacher's evaluation form p70**

	4	3	2	1
Creativity	Product has a very attractive and clear design. It presents an interesting style of clothes, with accurate information and very attractive images.	Product has an attractive and clear design. It presents an interesting style of clothes, with mostly accurate information and attractive images.	Product is attractive but with an unclear design. It presents an interesting style of clothes, but with some information and only one or two attractive images.	Product has an unattractive and unclear design. It presents an uninteresting style of clothes, with very little information and no attractive images.
Presentation skills	Speaks slowly, clearly and confidently. Is well prepared and knows what to say. Always looks at the audience and answers all questions.	Speaks slowly, clearly and confidently most of the time. Is quite well prepared and knows what to say most of the time. Usually looks at the audience and answers most questions.	Speaks slowly, clearly and confidently some of the time. Forgets what to say at times, so needs better preparation. Sometimes looks at the audience and answers some questions.	Doesn't speak clearly or confidently. Is unprepared and doesn't know what to say. Never looks at the audience or answers questions.

Cambridge Life Competencies Framework

You can also check students' progress in the following foundation layers.

FOUNDATION LAYERS	ABILITIES	ACTIONS
Digital Literacy	• Use digital tools	finding content from various sources, using online templates to create lookbook pages, sharing work online, using digital presentation techniques (e.g. webpages)
Discipline Knowledge	• Convince the audience	explaining and describing images, giving details, answering questions

○ Flipped classroom activities

Evaluate

In project groups, have students discuss their completed Peer-evaluation forms and ways to work better as a group. **> Peer-evaluation form p69**

Out of class: have students think about on their progress at home. **> My learning diary p68** **Production**

In class: hold a class discussion on what students know now, using the information from their learning diaries. **> My learning diary p68** **Production**

AN INFORMATION LEAFLET

- **Learning outcome:** make an information leaflet
- **Skills:** research and evaluate leaflets: research, select and organise facts about a (street) sport, decide which illustrations and photos to include
- **Resources:** two or more information leaflets, Information leaflet organiser p63, My time-management plan p71
- **Evaluation tools:** Information leaflet organiser p63, My time-management plan p71

 Student's Book pp78–79

Before you start

Collect two or three different types of leaflet to show students in class.

1 Preparation

Step 1: Introduce the topic

- Introduce the topic of information leaflets after the reading on Bossaball. p72

- Show students the leaflets. Encourage them to say what they are and who they are for. Ask: *What are information leaflets? What do they do? Why do people read them?*

- Explain that leaflets use short texts to give information. For example, they tell people about an event, or are used to sell something. Have students come up with some specific examples.

- Ask students to bring a leaflet to the next lesson (these don't need to be in English). They can discuss which leaflets they like / don't like and why.

Step 2: Analyse the model for the project 📖 pp78–79

- Complete **Exercises 1 to 3.**

Answers 1 2   2 Answers may vary.   3 1F 2F 3F 4T

- Ask questions about the leaflet, for example: *Why is there a photo on the leaflet? What are the people doing? What sections are in the leaflet and why? What information is in each section? Is the information useful?*

- Revise the language from the unit. Ask students to find examples of **comparatives and superlatives** in the leaflet.

 Critical Thinking
Synthesising ideas and information
Use the questions in Step 2 to assess how well students understand the format and presentation of information in leaflets.

Step 3: *How to* design a leaflet 📖 p78

- Go through the tips in **Exercise 4** with the class. Students say which ones are good pieces of advice. Ask students to give reasons for their answers. Have them use the leaflet model to find examples of items in the tips.

- 🎧 6.11 Play the audio for **Exercise 5**. Students check their answers in pairs or groups.

- Check answers with the class, correcting the bad advice, for example: *Use bright colours, not serious ones.* Check students understand that when they make their leaflets, they should use the tips in this *How to* section, including the corrected ones.

Answers b d e

Step 4: Clarify the project 📖 p79

- Follow the steps in > The learning stages of project work p10 .

- Brainstorm different sports and key information. Write ideas on the board.

- Have groups choose a sport for their leaflet and think of resources they could use (websites, sports centres, libraries, etc.).

> KWL chart p67   **Know and Want to know**

> Peer-evaluation form p69   **Preparation**

2 Development

Start this stage as soon as groups know their learning outcomes and what resources to use.

Step 1: Assign roles and responsibilities

- In project groups, have students choose general roles. **> Roles and responsibilities p16** Help them decide on further roles they can share, such as the ones in the diagram.

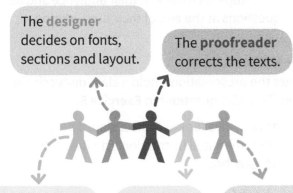

The **designer** decides on fonts, sections and layout.

The **proofreader** corrects the texts.

The **editor** makes the final decision on what content to include.

The **writer** produces the text.

The **picture manager** chooses the images.

⏱ Flipped classroom activities

Step 2: Research and analyse 📖 p79 ⏰ p71

Out of class: have groups do some of the PLAN section from **Exercise 6**, such as researching information and collecting images.

In class: monitor by asking the groups about their progress over a few classes.

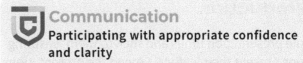

Communication
Participating with appropriate confidence and clarity

Monitor progress of the tasks in Step 3 to check how well students organise their leaflets.

Step 3: Draft and review 📖 p79 ⏰ p71

- Once groups have finished their research, have them complete the rest of the PLAN section. Hand out copies of the **> Information leaflet organiser p63** to help them plan their information. Tell them they can use this or any other organiser to put their notes together.

- Allow time for drafting and reviewing.

- Hold a class discussion about ways groups can improve their leaflets.

- Encourage group members to make improvements out of class. Have them bring their ideas to the next class for final preparation.

> Peer-evaluation form p69 **Development**

🔒 *Own it!* learning tip

Using social skills: giving opinions

Have group members share their opinions about what to include in their leaflets.
They should make a final decision. Monitor to help with useful language, for example: *I think, I'm not sure, I agree/don't agree, Good idea!* Encourage students to also use language for comparatives and superlatives when they give their opinions.

③ Production

Schedule presentation times and stick to them, ensuring all groups present their leaflets. Spread the presentations over a few classes, if necessary. Allow enough time for each presentation and for questions.

Before groups produce their final drafts, have them decide on the format and layouts for presenting their leaflet. 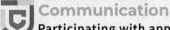 **> Presentation ideas p18**

As students complete their projects, check their abilities in the following Areas of Competency.

🛡 Critical Thinking
Synthesising ideas and information

Selects key points from diverse sources to create a new account and/or argument.

Evidence: **Different resources are used to select and present key information.**

🛡 Communication
Participating with appropriate confidence and clarity

Develops a clear description with a logical sequence of points.

Evidence: **Leaflet includes relevant information in each section.**

Uses a number of cohesive devices to link sentences into clear, coherent discourse.

Evidence: **Leaflet displays various techniques, such as sub-headings, bullets and lists.**

Step 1: Prepare 📖 p79 ⏱ p71

- Go through the checklist in the PRESENT section in **Exercise 7**.

- As groups prepare their project, remind them of the tasks they need to complete by asking them questions.

- Remind groups of the presentation date and how much time each group will have.

Step 2: Present 📖 p79

- For this project, we suggest one group member is the speaker. Have each group choose their speaker.

- Draw attention to the CHECK section from **Exercise 8**. Ask the class to think about these questions as they listen to each others' presentations.

- Have groups present their leaflets.

- Remind students to look at their audience and ask for questions at the end of their presentation.

Step 3: Reflect 📖 p81

- After the presentations, hold a class discussion on the CHECK questions in **Exercise 8**.

- Grade activities for this Reflect step, if necessary. (See Differentiated instruction activities below for further practice.)

Differentiated instruction

Support
Take into account each student's level when they reflect on their work and allow them to use L1 when making observations.
Consolidation
Have students make suggestions for improving their next presentation based on their discussion.
Extension
In pairs or groups, have students interview each other about what they know now. Tell them to list positive experiences and share them with the class.

> Peer-evaluation form p69   **Production**

🖱 Go to the digital collaboration space to set, track and assess students' work, or allow students to share and comment on their own work.

Project evaluation rubric: an information leaflet

Use these project-specific descriptors and your own choice of descriptors from the > Evaluation rubric p21 to check students individually or in groups. Make your own evaluation form. > Teacher's evaluation form p70

	4	3	2	1
Creativity	Product has a very original, attractive design. It uses bright photos and a clear font. It includes a map and contact details. It clearly focuses on the key information. The information is presented in a logical order.	Product has an original and attractive design. It uses bright photos and a clear font. It includes a map and contact details. It has some interesting facts. The information is presented in a logical order, except for one or two cases.	Product has a clear design that largely follows the model. It could use brighter photos and a clearer font. It includes a map or contact details. It has only one or two interesting facts. The information is understandable, but is presented in a random order.	Product has an unattractive design with little creativity and it doesn't follow the model. It needs more photos and it uses an unclear font. It is missing a map and contact details. It has no interesting facts. The information is not understandable.
Language use	Shows excellent use of language from unit (comparatives and superlatives). Project is understandable with only a few mistakes.	Shows good use of language from unit (comparatives and superlatives). Project is understandable with some mistakes.	Shows adequate use of language from unit (comparatives and superlatives). Project is understandable, but some sections need further explanation.	Doesn't use language from unit (comparatives and superlatives). Project is confusing and almost impossible to understand.

Cambridge Life Competencies Framework

You can also check students' progress in the following foundation layers.

FOUNDATION LAYERS	ABILITIES	ACTIONS
Digital Literacy	• Use digital tools	finding content on various websites, identifying appropriate content, checking facts with other digital sources, using digital tools to design the leaflet
Discipline Knowledge	• Convince the audience	explaining facts and images, giving details, summarising information, answering questions

Flipped classroom activities

Evaluate

In project groups, have students discuss their completed Peer-evaluation forms and ways to work better as a group. > Peer-evaluation form p69

Out of class: have students think about their progress at home. > KWL chart p67 **Learned**

In class: hold a class discussion on what students know now, using the information from their KWL charts. > KWL chart p67 **Learned**

A SCRAPBOOK

- **Learning outcome:** make a scrapbook
- **Skills:** research photos and information about them, describe photos, decide on a design and format, check each other's work
- **Resources:** scrapbook pages, Scrapbook organiser p64, My time-management plan p71
- **Evaluation tools:** Project evaluation rubric p49, My learning diary p68, Peer-evaluation form p69, Teacher's evaluation form p70

 Unit 7

Before you start
Collect examples of scrapbook pages (preferably from travel websites) to show students in class.

1 Preparation

Step 1: Introduce the topic

- Introduce the topic of scrapbooks after doing the language exercises. p87

- Show students the scrapbook pages. Ask: *What are these? Why do people keep scrapbooks? What do people keep in them? Do you keep a scrapbook?*

- Ask: *How is a scrapbook different from a photo album?* Explain that scrapbooks are different in that they also tell the stories behind the pictures. People keep other memorabilia in scrapbooks, such as tickets or leaflets.

- Ask students each to find an example of a scrapbook online to bring to the next class (in their own language or English). They can describe the scrapbooks in groups.

Step 2: Analyse the model for the project 🔘 Unit 7

- Have students describe the pictures in the model scrapbook. Ask: *What is this scrapbook about?* Then students read the texts.

- Check comprehension. Ask: *Which festival/animals did they see? What do they say about the Altai Mountains? What is interesting for you? Why?*

- Grade activities for this step, if necessary. (See Differentiated instruction activities below for further practice.)

Differentiated instruction

Support
Have students find examples of the past tense in the scrapbook and categorise the verbs into regular and irregular.
Consolidation
Have students complete some gapped sentences from the scrapbook with the past simple form of the verbs.
Extension
Have students write an extra sentence about each picture in the scrapbook, using the past tense.

Step 3: *How to* design a scrapbook 🔘 Unit 7

- Go through the *How to* tips with the class. Different students say why each idea is important.

- Check students understand that when they design their scrapbooks, they should use the ideas in this *How to* section.

🛡 **Creative Thinking**
Creating new content from own ideas or other resources
Remind students that scrapbooks use photos and pictures as prompts to tell a story. Review other prompts scrapbooks use (e.g. concert/theatre/bus tickets, leaflets, small objects).

Step 4: Clarify the project 🔘 Unit 7

- Follow the steps in > The learning stages of project work p10 .

- Brainstorm parts of the world students would like to visit. Write a list on the board.

- Have groups think about what they can see and do in each place and make notes.

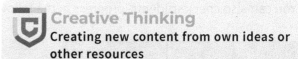

> My learning diary p68   **Preparation**
> Peer-evaluation form p69   **Preparation**

② Development

Start this stage as soon as groups know their learning outcomes and have brainstormed ideas for places.

Step 1: Assign roles and responsibilities

- In project groups, have students choose the general roles. **> Roles and responsibilities p16** Help them decide on further roles they can share, such as:

The **researcher** helps find information about the topic.

The **digital editor** manages the presentation of digital formats.

The **archivist** helps find memorabilia.

The **picture manager** helps find and choose the pictures.

The **proofreader** checks the texts.

Step 2: Research and analyse ⬉ Unit 7 🕐 p71

- Have groups start the P L A N section from **Exercise 1** and choose a place from the brainstormed list in the Preparation stage.
- Groups decide on design and format (digital or paper). Say that there are free scrapbook makers online.
- Hand out copies of the **> Scrapbook organiser p64** to each student.

🕐 Flipped classroom activities

Out of class: have students find photos related to their place and categorise them in their organisers. Have them research each photo or item and make notes in the spidergrams.

In class: have groups put together their information and decide who will prepare each section.

🔒 *Own it!* learning tip

Disagreeing appropriately

If students cannot agree on who will prepare each section, or don't like some of the material their group members want to include, encourage polite discussion and allow them to give their opinions explaining their reasons. Have them make alternative suggestions. Monitor to help with useful language, for example: *I'm not sure about ... Why don't we ... ? I disagree because ...*

🛡 Social Responsibilities
Understanding and describing own and others' cultures

Ask groups to compare the culture they are researching with their own. Discuss ideas.

🕐 Flipped classroom activities

Step 3: Draft and review ⬉ Unit 7 🕐 p71

Out of class: group members complete the rest of the P L A N section in **Exercise 1** by preparing their section.

In class: have group members check each other's sections. Encourage groups to make a final decision on the design.

Out of class: if groups are working digitally, they could share and check their sections online.

> My learning diary p68 Development

> Peer-evaluation form p69 Development

③ Production

Schedule presentation times and stick to them. In this case, a group presents their scrapbook to another group, so all presentations could be scheduled for one class. Allow enough time for feedback and questions.

If groups are not using a digital scrapbook maker, they may want to present their work as a poster or webpage.

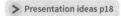 Presentation ideas p18

As students complete their projects, check their abilities in the following Areas of Competency.

Creative Thinking
Creating new content from own ideas or other resources

Writes or tells an original story, given prompts or without prompts.

Evidence: **Scrapbook visuals are described in an original way.**

Makes up own 'what if' activities and brings others in.

Evidence: **Students discuss different possibilities for what to include and brainstorm alternative situations.**

Social Responsibilities
Understanding and describing own and others' cultures

Accepts others and shows respect for cultural difference.

Evidence: **Scrapbook includes positive descriptions of different cultures.**

Understands the contributions of different cultures to their own lives.

Evidence: **Scrapbook presentation relates different cultures to the students' own.**

Step 1: Prepare 🖰 Unit 7 ⏱ p71

- Go through the checklist in the PRESENT section in **Exercise 2**.

- As students prepare their sections, ask questions, for example: *Are there photos and other memorabilia? Do you all agree on the format? Are you describing past events?* Help with language as necessary.

- Let groups discuss ways of presenting pictures with different fonts and bright colours. Remind them to disagree politely.

Step 2: Present 🖰 Unit 7

- Draw attention to the CHECK section in **Exercise 3**. Ask the class to think about these questions as they listen to each others' presentations.

- Remind students to look at their audience and ask for questions at the end of their presentation.

- Pairs of groups get together and present their scrapbooks to each other.

- Tell the class to make notes on what they like about the different scrapbooks.

Step 3: Reflect 🖰 Unit 7

- After the presentations, hold a class discussion on the CHECK questions in **Exercise 3**.

- Have the class say what they like about each scrapbook and why. Ask: *What new things do you know now about the different places?*

- Encourage students to think about each stage of the project process, including positive experiences and things they could improve.

> Peer-evaluation form p69   **Production**

🖰 Go to the digital collaboration space to set, track and assess students' work, or allow students to share and comment on their own work.

Project evaluation rubric: a scrapbook

Use these project-specific descriptors and your own choice of descriptors from the **> Evaluation rubric p21** to check students individually or in groups. Make your own evaluation form. **> Teacher's evaluation form p70**

	4	3	2	1
Creativity	Product has a very attractive design with bright colours and clear fonts. It has a very interesting topic with very attractive visuals. It has many original descriptions for the visuals.	Product has an attractive design with bright colours and mostly clear fonts. It has an interesting topic with attractive visuals. It has some original descriptions for the visuals.	Product has an attractive design, but the fonts are not clear. It has a fairly interesting topic with some attractive visuals. It has a few original descriptions for the visuals.	Product has an unattractive and unclear design. It has an uninteresting topic with unattractive visuals. It doesn't have any original descriptions for the visuals.
Language use	Excellent use of language from unit (past simple). Product contains a wide range of regular and irregular verbs. Project is understandable with only a few mistakes.	Good use of language from unit (past simple). Product contains a range of regular and irregular verbs. Project is understandable with some mistakes.	Adequate use of language from unit (past simple). Product contains a limited range of regular and irregular verbs. Project is understandable, but some sections need further explanation.	Poor or no use of language from unit (past simple). Product contains very few regular or irregular verbs. Project is poorly written.

 Cambridge Life Competencies Framework
You can also check students' progress in the following foundation layers.

FOUNDATION LAYERS	ABILITIES	ACTIONS
Digital Literacy	• Use digital tools	finding content from various sources, using digital scrapbook makers to create scrapbook pages, sharing work online
Discipline Knowledge	• Convince the audience	describing images, places and events, giving details, answering questions

⟳ Flipped classroom activities

Evaluate

In project groups, have students discuss their completed Peer-evaluation forms and ways to work better as a group. **> Peer-evaluation form p69**

Out of class: have students think about on their progress at home. **> My learning diary p68** **Production**

In class: hold a class discussion on what students learned, using the information from their learning diaries. **> My learning diary p68** **Production**

AN INTERVIEW

> - **Learning outcome:** interview someone about their life in the past
> - **Skills:** choose a person and get photos about them, prepare questions, interview the person
> - **Resources:** recorded or written interviews, recording equipment (phones and/or pen and paper), Interview organiser p65, My time-management plan p71
> - **Evaluation tools:** Project evaluation rubric p53, KWL chart p67, Peer-evaluation form p69, Teacher's evaluation form p70
>
>   Student's Book pp102–103

Before you start

Find two interviews about the past in magazines, newspapers or on the internet to show students in class. These can be recorded or written.

Preparation

Step 1: Introduce the topic

- Introduce the topic of interviews after doing the grammar exercises. p99

- Show students the interviews, or have them listen to them. Ask: *Who is interviewing who? What questions does the interviewer ask? What is the interview about?*

- Explain that an interview is a conversation where an interviewer asks questions and an interviewee answers them. People do interviews to get information.

- Ask students each to bring an example of an interview to the next class, preferably in English. They can discuss where they found them and what they are about.

Step 2: Analyse the model for the project pp102–103

- Complete **Exercises 1** to **3**. Play the audio for **Exercises 2** and **3** and check answers.

  Answers **1** Students' own answers **2** They are about Clarissa's life when she was a child. **3 2** It was simple and she was happy. **3** Houses and a post office. **4** She ran away. **5** Family, friends and memories.

- Ask questions about the model interview: *What do Ruby and Jacob want to find out? What questions do they ask?* Play Track 8.11 again if necessary.

- 8.12 Complete **Exercise 4**. Play the audio and check.

  Answers **4** Closed, open and follow-up questions.

- Ask students to look at the model interview questions and review how to form **past simple Wh- questions**. Then they complete **Exercise 5**.

  Answers **5** They are open and follow-up questions.

 Collaboration
Listening respectfully and responding constructively to others' contributions or activities

Draw attention to how the interviewers respond to the interviewee with a follow-up question *(Who was Cookie?)*. Encourage students to listen actively and carefully throughout their project.

Step 3: *How to* do a recorded interview p102

- Go through the *How to* tips in **Exercise 6** with the class. Students classify them in the table.

  Answers **6** Before the interview: c, g; During the interview: a, b, d, e, h; After the interview: f

- Have students discuss the question in **Exercise 7**. Ask them to give examples or reasons for their answers. You can play Track 8.11 again, pausing when there is evidence that Ruby or Jacob followed the tips.

- Remind students that when they do their interviews, they should use the ideas in this *How to* section.

Step 4: Clarify the project pp102–103

- Follow the steps in > The learning stages of project work p10 . Note that for this project, students will work in pairs.

- Brainstorm people students can interview, such as friends, family or teachers. Ideally, the interview should be in English, so encourage students to think of people that speak this language. If they don't know anyone who does, as a last resort they can interview you, or each other.

- Have pairs list topics they can ask questions about. Tell them to bring their lists to the next class

> KWL chart p67   **Know and Want to know**

> Peer-evaluation form p69   **Preparation**

② Development

Start this stage as soon as groups know their learning outcomes and have a list of possible interviewees.

Step 1: Assign roles and responsibilities

- In pairs, have students decide on roles they can share during and after the interview. Help them with some ideas, such as the ones in the table.

During the interview

The interviewer asks the questions and responds to answers.

The sound engineer records the interview; or the note-taker makes notes of the answers.

After the interview

The editor suggests which parts of the interview to use.

The writer types or writes up the interview.

Both members write and send the thank you email / letter.

Step 2: Research and analyse p103 p71

- Have pairs choose the person to interview. Remind them that ideally this person should speak English. Tell them to contact them and agree on a time.

- Hand out a copy of the > Interview organiser p65 to each pair.

- Have students go through the PLAN section in **Exercise 8**. Ask them to write the open questions in their organisers, as well as phrases they can use during and after the interview.

- Grade activities for this step, if necessary. (See Differentiated instruction activities above for further practice.)

Differentiated instruction

Support
Help students with language as they prepare their questions. Check use of the past simple.
Consolidation
Encourage a variety of *Wh-* questions. Say that open questions are more useful for interviews because you can get more information.
Extension
Have students prepare some follow-up questions in advance.

⟳ Flipped classroom activities

Step 3: Draft and review 📖 p103 🕐 p71

Out of class: have pairs do their interviews. Remind them of their roles as interviewer and sound engineer or note-taker. Tell them to take their Interview organisers and recording equipment (phones, notepads, etc.).

In class: pairs write and edit their interviews using their recordings or notes.

Pairs write and send a thank you email or letter to their interviewee, together with a copy of the interview. Then they complete the checklist in their organisers.

🛡 Critical Thinking
Evaluating ideas, arguments and options

Monitor pairs' comprehension of their interviewee's answers. Encourage them to identify questions about facts, opinions and assumptions in their interviews, such as: *What happened? What did you think? What was it like?*

> Peer-evaluation form p69   **Development**

③ Production

Schedule presentation times and stick to them, ensuring all pairs present their interviews. Allow enough time for students to read or listen to each other's interviews.

Before groups produce their final projects, have them decide on the format for presenting their interview: written, audio or both.

As students complete their projects, check their abilities in the following Areas of Competency.

Critical Thinking
Evaluating ideas, arguments and options

Distinguishes between fact and opinion.

Evidence: Interview has questions about facts, opinions and feelings.

Identifies assumptions and inferences in an argument.

Evidence: Interview has questions asking for reasons and points of view.

Collaboration
Listening respectfully and responding constructively to others' contributions or activities

Is ready to justify, adapt and abandon a proposal in response to others' queries and contributions.

Evidence: Students adapted follow-up questions or changed the topic depending on what the interviewee said.

Listens to, acknowledges different points of view, respectfully.

Evidence: Students paid attention and interacted with the interviewee politely.

Step 1: Prepare 📖 p103 ⏰ p71

- Go through the checklist in the PRESENT section in **Exercise 9**.

- As pairs prepare their project, ask questions, for example: *Do you have photos of the person/places? Where can you find old photos of ... ? Did you send your interviewee a thank you email?*

- Remind pairs of the presentation date and how much time each group will have.

Step 2: Present 📖 p103

- Have students do the PRESENT section in **Exercise 9**. Pairs can play their recordings or display their written interviews then answer questions.

- Draw attention to the CHECK section in **Exercise 10**. Ask the class to think about these questions as they listen to or read each others' interviews.

- Encourage students to ask each other questions, for example: *What did you learn about the past? What did your person think about ... ? Why did things change for him/her?*

Step 3: Reflect 📖 p103

- After the presentations, hold a class discussion on the CHECK questions in **Exercise 10**.

- Encourage students to think about each stage of the project process, including positive experiences and things they could improve. They can also share what they found interesting about life in the past.

🔄 *Own it!* learning tip

Sharing resources

As students discuss their projects in Step 3, encourage them to think about the resources they used and shared. Ask: *Did you have everything you needed to do your interview? Whose equipment did you use? Did you lend or borrow anything?* Say that it's a good idea to share resources in order to complete or improve projects.

> Peer-evaluation form p69   **Production**

🔖 Go to the digital collaboration space to set, track and assess students' work, or allow students to share and comment on their own work.

Project evaluation rubric: an interview

Use these project-specific descriptors and your own choice of descriptors from the [> Evaluation rubric p21] to check students individually or in groups. Make your own evaluation form. [> Teacher's evaluation form p70]

	4	3	2	1
Creativity	Product has a clear and imaginative purpose. Questions are varied and interesting. Answers include very interesting facts and opinions. Has a wide variety of photos of the person and place.	Product has a clear purpose. Most questions are varied and interesting. Answers include some interesting facts and opinions. Has a variety of photos of the person and place.	Product has a purpose but some parts are not related to it. Some questions are interesting, but there is little variety. Answers include one or two interesting facts and opinions. Has few photos of the person and place.	Product doesn't show a clear purpose. Questions are not varied, or interesting. Answers do not include any interesting facts or opinions. Doesn't have photos of the person or place.
Language use	Excellent use of language from unit (past simple questions). Always uses polite language with the interviewee. Project is understandable with only a few mistakes.	Good use of language from unit (past simple questions). Mostly uses polite language with the interviewee. Project is understandable with some mistakes.	Adequate use of language from unit (past simple questions). Uses some polite language with the interviewee. Project is understandable, but some sections need further explanation.	Poor or no use of language from unit (past simple questions). Doesn't use polite language with the interviewee. Project is confusing and almost impossible to understand.

Cambridge Life Competencies Framework

You can also check students' progress in the following foundation layers.

FOUNDATION LAYERS	ABILITIES	ACTIONS
Emotional Development and Wellbeing	• Empathise and build relationships	listening respectfully and responding appropriately, paying attention to others' feelings, encouraging others to verbalise emotions
Digital Literacy	• Use digital tools	creating recordings, sharing work and resources online (e.g. audio files)

Flipped classroom activities

Evaluate

In project groups, have students discuss their completed Peer-evaluation forms and ways to work better as a group. [> Peer-evaluation form p69]

Out of class: have students think about on their progress at home. [> KWL chart p67] **Learned**

In class: hold a class discussion on what students know now, using the information from their KWL charts. [> KWL chart p67] **Learned**

9 THE CULTURE PROJECT

A WEBPAGE

- **Learning outcome:** make a summer camp webpage
- **Skills:** research information and use a spidergram to organise it, use a webpage template, prepare and check each other's sections
- **Resources:** two or more webpages about summer camps, Webpage organiser p66, My time-management plan p71
- **Evaluation tools:** Project evaluation rubric p57, My learning diary p68, Peer-evaluation form p69, Teacher's evaluation form p70

 Unit 9

Before you start
Find two or three examples of summer camp webpages to show students in class.

1 Preparation

Step 1: Introduce the topic

- Introduce the topic of webpages after doing the reading exercises. p108 Show students the webpages. Ask: *What are they about? What information is in each section? Who are the webpages for? Are they interesting? Why / Why not?*

- Ask students which webpages they visit and what for. Ask: *What are they about?*

- Ask students each to bring an example of a webpage about a different summer camp to the next class. They can discuss the webpages in groups.

Learning to Learn
Taking control of your own learning
Ask students to bring examples of useful sources to the next class.

Step 2: Analyse the model for the project Unit 9

- Have students look at the sections, titles and pictures on the model webpage. Ask: *What is this webpage about?* Then students read the webpage.

- Check comprehension. Ask: *Who is the Crazy Cook Camp for? When and where is it? What can you do and what will you learn? Would you like to go on this camp?*

- Ask questions about the webpage's design and purpose: *Is it attractive? What is it about?*

- Grade activities for this step, if necessary. (See Differentiated instruction activities below for further practice.)

Differentiated instruction

Support
Have students find five predictions about the future on the webpage.
Consolidation
Have students complete gapped sentences from the webpage with the correct form of *will* + verb.
Extension
Tell students they are going on the camp. Have them write five plans using *be going to*.

Step 3: *How to* make a webpage Unit 9

- Go through the *How to* tips with the class. Different students say why each idea is important.

- Ensure students understand that when they make their webpages, they should use the ideas in this *How to* section.

Step 4: Clarify the project Unit 9

- Follow the steps in > The learning stages of project work p10 .

- Brainstorm places to go on a summer camp. Then ask: *What activities can you do in each place?*

- Have groups discuss sources where they can find out more about the places and summer camp activities.

> My learning diary p68 **Preparation**

> Peer-evaluation form p69 **Preparation**

2 Development

Start this stage as soon as groups know their learning outcomes and what sources to use.

Step 1: Assign roles and responsibilities

- In project groups, have students choose general roles.
  > **Roles and responsibilities p16** Help them decide on further roles they can share, such as those in the diagram.

The **camp organiser** helps choose activities.

The **marketing manager** ensures the webpage is attractive and persuasive.

The **camp administrator** suggests places, dates and times.

The **web designer** supervises the webpage design.

The **editor** checks that texts and pictures fit in each section.

Step 2: Research and analyse Unit 9 p71

- Have groups start the PLAN section in **Exercise 1**. Have them decide on their summer camp and give it a name.

- Once students have made notes for the ideas in the notebook page, hand out a copy of the
  > **Webpage organiser p66** to each student. Students use the spidergram to organise their notes.

- Point to the webpage designs in the second part of the organiser. Encourage groups to look for different online templates and sketch a design in the space provided.

- Groups work together to organise their information. Then they agree on who will prepare each section.

🖐 *Own it!* learning tip

Sharing resources

Have group leaders manage the tasks and create specific roles. Say that group members can be given a section or volunteer for one. Monitor to help with useful language, for example: *Why don't you … ? I can … Let's … You're good at …*

○ Flipped classroom activities

Step 3: Draft and review ⬆ Unit 9 ⏰ p71

Out of class: have group members prepare their parts as explained in the PLAN section.

Encourage students to check facts about their summer camps in their sources.

In class: group members check each other's sections. If they haven't done so yet, groups decide on final design and content.

Out of class: led by the web designer, have groups work on the design and share and check their work online. Remind them to use a template that matches their chosen design.

🛡 Creative Thinking
Participating in creative activities
Encourage all students to get involved in the creative process, from finding information to designing the webpage.

> **My learning diary p68** Development
> **Peer-evaluation form p69** Development

③ Production

Schedule presentation times and stick to them, so that all groups can present their webpage on a big screen. Spread the presentations over a few classes, if necessary. Allow enough time for each presentation and for questions.

Before groups produce their final webpages, help them follow the online steps for the template they have chosen to complete their project.

> Presentation ideas p18

As students complete their projects, check their abilities in the following Areas of Competency.

🛡 Learning to Learn
Taking control of your own learning

Finds sources of information and help.

Evidence: Students work together online and in class to share sources.

Reviews vocabulary regularly and systematically.

Evidence: Students make final language corrections to their webpage.

🛡 Creative Thinking
Participating in creative activities

Encourages group members to make activities more original.

Evidence: Webpage includes interesting activities.

Participates in activities that include creative thinking.

Evidence: Group members decide on design and content to produce a creative webpage.

Step 1: Prepare 🖱 Unit 9 ⏱ p71

- Go through the checklist in the PRESENT section in **Exercise 2**.

- As groups prepare their project, ask questions, for example: *Is your webpage easy to use? What sections does it have? Is there anything missing?*

⟳ Flipped classroom activities

Out of class: groups finalise their webpages by sharing tasks online. Remind them to follow the ideas in the *How to* section.

In class: groups make final corrections. Have them focus on both the overall look and the language: they should check grammar, vocabulary, spelling and punctuation.

Step 2: Present 🖱 Unit 9

- Draw attention to the CHECK section in **Exercise 3**. Ask the class to think about these questions as they look at each others' webpages.

- If possible, have groups project their webpages on a big screen. Check that each group member presents their section.

- After the presentations, students could try and use the webpages: they could click on the different features, zoom in, etc.

- Encourage students to ask questions and make notes about what they like.

Step 3: Reflect 🖱 Unit 9

- After the presentations, hold a class discussion on the CHECK questions in **Exercise 3**.

- Have the class say what they liked about each webpage and why. Then ask: *Which summer camps would you like to go on?* Finally, the class can vote on the best webpage.

- Encourage students to think about each stage of the project process, including positive experiences and things they could improve.

> Peer-evaluation form p69   **Production**

🖱 Go to the digital collaboration space to set, track and assess students' work, or allow students to share and comment on their own work.

Project evaluation rubric: a webpage

Use these project-specific descriptors and your own choice of descriptors from the ❯ Evaluation rubric p21 to check students individually or in groups. Make your own evaluation form. ❯ Teacher's evaluation form p70

	4	3	2	1
Creativity	Product's name is very original. Product is attractive and contains visuals for each description. It is easy to use and understand. It is very well organised and includes all the important information.	Product's name is interesting. Product is attractive and contains visuals for most descriptions. It is generally easy to use and understand. It is well organised and includes most of the important information.	Product's name is relevant, but not interesting. Only some parts are attractive, and a few descriptions don't contain visuals. Some parts are difficult to use or understand. It is organised, but doesn't include some important information.	Product's name is not interesting. Product is unattractive with very few visuals. It is impossible to use or understand. It is disorganised and doesn't include any important information.
Language use	Excellent use of language from unit (the future; summer camp activities). Project is understandable with only a few mistakes.	Good use of language from unit (the future; summer camp activities). Project is understandable with some mistakes.	Adequate use of language from unit (the future; summer camp activities). Project is understandable but some sections need further explanation.	Poor or no use of language from unit (the future; summer camp activities). Project is poorly written.

 Cambridge Life Competencies Framework
You can also check students' progress in the following foundation layers.

FOUNDATION LAYERS	ABILITIES	ACTIONS
Digital Literacy	• Use digital tools	finding content, creating a webpage, sharing work online, using digital presentation techniques, adding interactive features
Discipline Knowledge	• Convince the audience	explaining facts and images, describing activities, giving details, answering questions

⟳ Flipped classroom activities

Evaluate

In project groups, have students discuss their completed Peer-evaluation forms and ways to work better as a group. ❯ Peer-evaluation form p69

Out of class: have students think about on their progress at home. ❯ My learning diary p68 **Production**

In class: hold a class discussion on what students learned, using the information from their learning diaries. ❯ My learning diary p68 **Production**

POSTER ORGANISER

Name of festival

What?

Where?

How many people?

When?

Activities

Interesting information

Ideas for images (flags, maps, people, etc.)

CLASS SURVEY ORGANISER

Title		Bar chart
Topic question		
Total number of students		

Activities	Number of students
1	
2	
3	
4	
5	
6	

Summary of results

Conclusions

HAIKU ORGANISER

Topic	Picture or drawing of topic
How the topic makes me feel	

Topic words

My haiku

Haiku syllables

PHOTOCOPIABLE

FOOD TRUCK ORGANISER

Illustration ideas
(drawings)

Name

Illustration ideas
(drawings)

Menu
(Include main dishes, specials, sweets, drinks, special offers and prices.)

LOOKBOOK ORGANISER

Spidergram

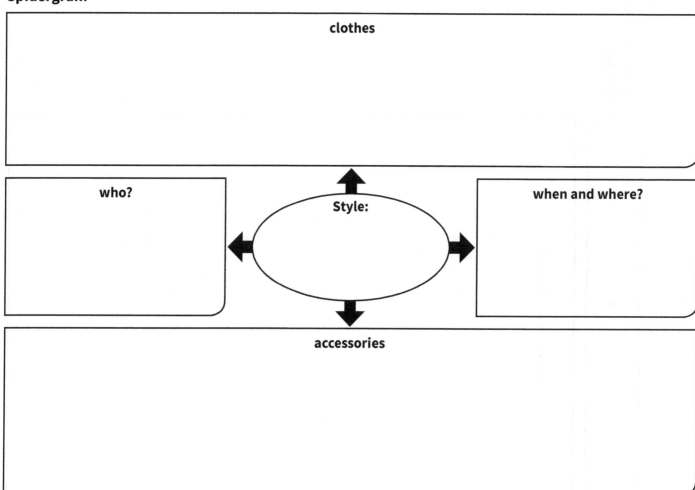

clothes

who?

Style:

when and where?

accessories

LOOKBOOK TEMPLATE

Use this template to organise your lookbook page.

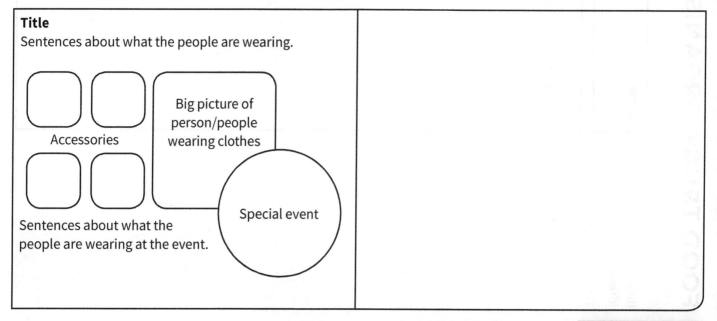

Title
Sentences about what the people are wearing.

Accessories

Big picture of person/people wearing clothes

Special event

Sentences about what the people are wearing at the event.

INFORMATION LEAFLET ORGANISER

Name of sport		Equipment		Benefits
Description (What is it?)				
Time and place to do the sport (Where and when?)		Is it a team sport? What do the teams do?		Interesting facts
Who can do/play the sport?		Rules		Contact details
Ideas for images (photos, maps, illustrations)				

SCRAPBOOK ORGANISER

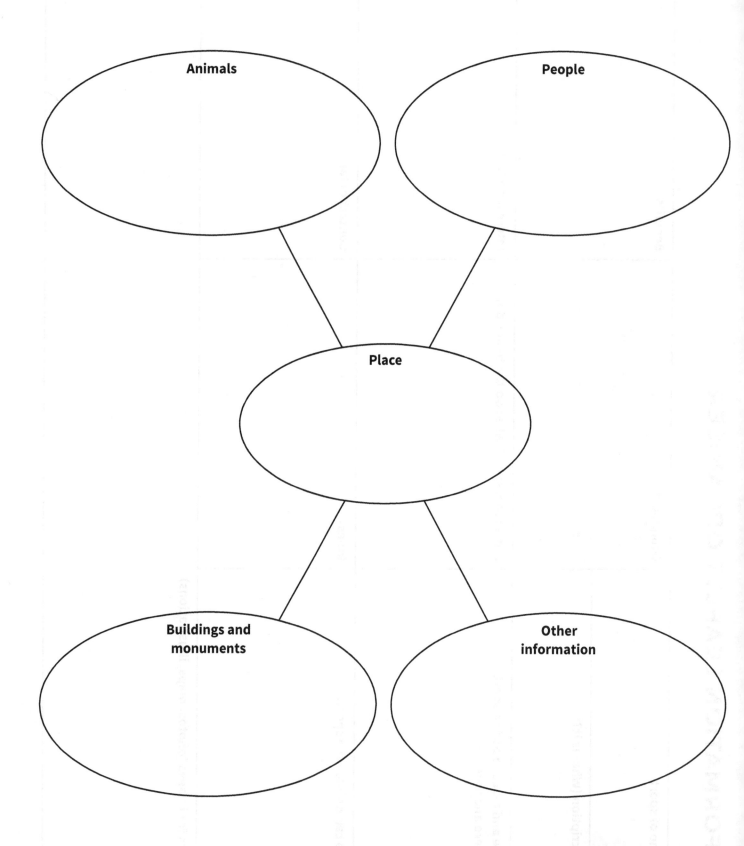

Animals

People

Place

Buildings and
monuments

Other
information

INTERVIEW ORGANISER

Name of person: _____ Date, time and place: _____

1 Before the interview, prepare open questions about the person's life in the past. During the interview, add any follow-up questions you think about.

1 _____ Follow-up: _____

2 _____ Follow-up: _____

3 _____ Follow-up: _____

4 _____ Follow-up: _____

5 _____ Follow-up: _____

6 _____ Follow-up: _____

Write phrases to use during the interview.
Introducing yourself:

Explaining why you're doing the interview:

Write phrases to use after the interview.
Saying thank you:

---

2 Complete the checklist.

Before the interview, I …	✓
planned the questions and time.	
checked my equipment.	
During the interview, I …	✓
introduced myself and explained the purpose.	
recorded answers and made notes.	
listened carefully.	
After the interview, I …	✓
thanked the person.	
typed or wrote up the interview.	
sent the person a copy and thank you email / letter.	

WEBPAGE ORGANISER

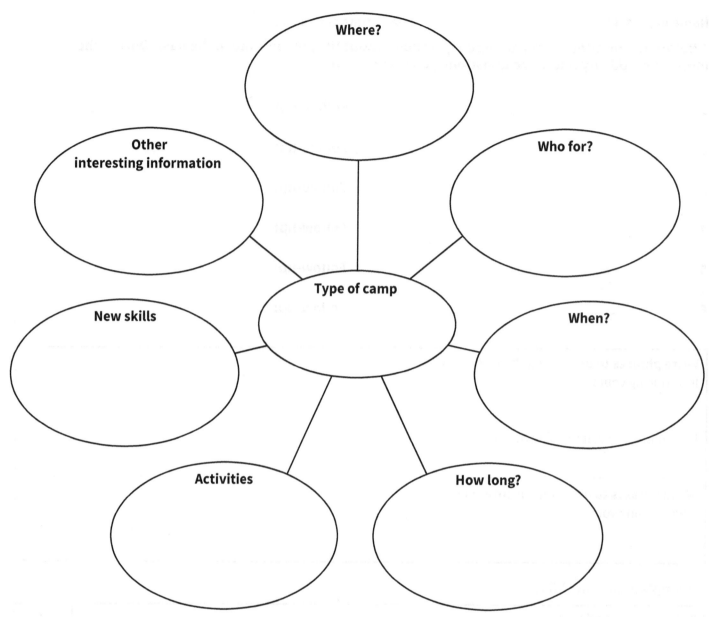

Where?

Other interesting information

Who for?

Type of camp

New skills

When?

Activities

How long?

Look at the webpage designs. Then draw your own design including all the information in your spidergram.

© Cambridge University Press 2020 Unit 9 Webpage organiser **PHOTOCOPIABLE**

Name: _____

Date: _____

Unit, topic and project: _____

KWL CHART

Know	Want to know	Learned (Know now)
What do we know about the topic?	*What do we want to know about the topic?*	*What do we know now about the topic?*
		What do we know now about the tasks?
What are our tasks?		*What can we do now as a group?*

© Cambridge University Press 2020 Unit 2 Class survey organiser

Name: _____

Date: _____

Unit, topic and project: _____

MY LEARNING DIARY

1 PREPARATION

- What am I learning?   • What can I use? (for example, the internet, the library, magazines …)
- Who is in my project group?   • What is my role in the group?

2 DEVELOPMENT

- What is difficult about this project?   • Who or what can help me?   • What do I like / don't I like?
- How can we make our work better?

3 PRODUCTION

- Is it a good presentation? Why / Why not?   • In the presentation, what is my role?
- How do I feel when I give a presentation?

Name: _____

Date: _____

Unit, topic and project: _____

PEER-EVALUATION FORM

1 In your group, evaluate your performance. Mark (✓) the columns.

1 PREPARATION	☺	😐	☹
We listen to the instructions.			
We understand the project.			

2 DEVELOPMENT	☺	😐	☹
We do our best in the project.			
We work well as a group.			

3 PRODUCTION	☺	😐	☹
We answer questions about our work.			
We ask questions about others' work.			

2 Write one good thing about this project.

_____

_____

_____

3 How can your group work better in the next project? Write one idea.

_____

_____

_____

_____

Name: _____

Date: _____

Unit, topic and project: _____

TEACHER'S EVALUATION FORM

Group or individual performance grades for the selected ✓ general areas.
Grades are as follows: 4 = Exceeds expectations; 3 = Very good, 2 = Good, 1 = Needs improvement.

✓	Areas / Outcomes	Grade	✓	Areas / Outcomes	Grade
	Learning outcomes			Creativity	
	Planning and organisation			Problem-solving skills	
	Use of information and resources			Language use	
	Collaboration (Teamwork)			Presentation skills	
	Time management			Final product	

Group or individual performance grades for the project-specific areas.
Grades are as follows: 4 = Exceeds expectations, 3 = Very good, 2 = Good, 1 = Needs improvement.

Project-specific area	Grade
1	
2	
3	
4	
5	

🛡 The Cambridge Life Competencies Framework

[Student's name / Group] _____ showed (✓) did not show (✗)
development in the following competencies and skills during this project.

Competency 1	✓ / ✗	Foundation layers	✓ / ✗
		Emotional Development and Wellbeing	
		Digital Literacy	
Competency 2	✓ / ✗	Discipline Knowledge	
		Comments:	
Comments:			

Overall grade: _____

General comments:

Area(s) of improvement:

Name: _____

Date: _____

Unit, topic and project: _____

MY TIME-MANAGEMENT PLAN

What tasks do you need to do for each step? Write them below, and write the time prediction. Then tick (✓) each task as you complete it and write the actual time it takes.

Research and analyse

What do I need to do?	Time prediction	Actual time
1 ☐ _____	→ 🕐 _____	→ 🕐 _____
2 ☐ _____	→ 🕐 _____	→ 🕐 _____
3 ☐ _____	→ 🕐 _____	→ 🕐 _____

Draft and review

What do I need to do?	Time prediction	Actual time
1 ☐ _____	→ 🕐 _____	→ 🕐 _____
2 ☐ _____	→ 🕐 _____	→ 🕐 _____
3 ☐ _____	→ 🕐 _____	→ 🕐 _____

Prepare

What do I need to do?	Time prediction	Actual time
1 ☐ _____	→ 🕐 _____	→ 🕐 _____
2 ☐ _____	→ 🕐 _____	→ 🕐 _____
3 ☐ _____	→ 🕐 _____	→ 🕐 _____

Reflect

Think about these points.

- I manage my time well during my project work.   ☐ Yes.   ☐ Can be better.
- I have time to complete self-evaluation tools for each stage.   ☐ Yes.   ☐ No.
- How can I improve my time management in the next project?

_____

_____

Acknowledgements

The authors and publishers acknowledge the following sources of copyright material and are grateful for the permissions granted. While every effort has been made, it has not always been possible to identify the sources of all the material used, or to trace all copyright holders. If any omissions are brought to our notice, we will be happy to include the appropriate acknowledgements on reprinting and in the next update to the digital edition, as applicable.

Key: Int = Introduction.

Photography

The following photographs are sourced from Getty Images.
Int: Hero Images; bonniej/E+; MachineHeadz/iStock/Getty Images Plus; code6d/E+; ilyast/DigitalVision Vectors; Snapshots from *Own It Student's Book 1 pp. 54, 78, 79;* FatCamera/E+; RobinOlimb/DigitalVision Vectors; RaStudio/iStock/Getty Images Plus; Wavebreakmedia/iStock/Getty Images Plus; Snapshots from *Own It Teacher's Resource Bank 1 Cultural Project 1;* SpiffyJ/DigitalVision Vectors.

The following photograph is sourced from other library.
Int: Kirby Wu.

Typesetting: TXT Servicios editoriales

Cover design and illustration: Collaborate Agency.

Editing: Andrew Reid